Twayne's New Critical Introductions
to Shakespeare

THE MERCHANT
OF VENICE

Twayne's New Critical Introductions to Shakespeare

THE MERCHANT OF VENICE

John Lyon

Lecturer in English, University of Bristol

Twayne Publishers · Boston
A Division of G. K. Hall & Co.

Published in the United States by Twayne Publishers,
division of G. K. Hall & Co.,
70 Lincoln Street, Boston, Massachusetts.

Published simultaneously in Great Britain by
Harvester · Wheatsheaf,
66 Wood Lane End, Hemel Hempstead, Hertfordshire.

Library of Congress Cataloging-in-Publication Data
Lyon, John, 1933–
    The Merchant of Venice / John Lyon.
       p.   cm. — (Twayne's new critical introductions to
  Shakespeare)
    Bibliography: p.
    Includes index.
    ISBN 0–8057–8708–9.   ISBN 0–8057–8712–7 (pbk.)
    [1. Shakespeare, William, 1564–1616. Merchant of
Venice.]
    I. Title.   II. Series.
    PR2825.L96 1988
    822.3′3—dc19   88–16466
                                               CIP

To
Matthew and Sarah Addison

Titles in the Series

GENERAL EDITOR: GRAHAM BRADSHAW

General Editor's Preface

The *New Critical Introductions to Shakespeare* series will include studies of all Shakespeare's plays, together with two volumes on the non-dramatic verse, and is designed to offer a challenge to all students of Shakespeare.

Each volume will be brief enough to read in an evening, but long enough to avoid those constraints which are inevitable in articles and short essays. Each contributor will develop a sustained critical reading of the play in question, which addresses those difficulties and critical disagreements which each play has generated.

Different plays present different problems, different challenges and excitements. In isolating these, each volume will present a preliminary survey of the play's stage history and critical reception. The volumes then provide a more extended discussion of these matters in the main text, and of matters relating to genre, textual problems and the use of source material, or to historical and theoretical issues. But here, rather than setting a row of dragons at the gate, we have assumed that 'background' should figure only as it emerges into a critical foreground; part of the critical endeavour is to establish, and sift, those issues which seem most pressing.

So, for example, when Shakespeare determined that *his* Othello and Desdemona should have no time to live together, or that Cordelia dies while Hermione survives, his

vii

deliberate departures from his source material have a critical significance which is often blurred, when discussed in the context of lengthily detailed surveys of 'the sources'. Alternatively, plays like *The Merchant of Venice* or *Measure for Measure* show Shakespeare welding together different 'stories' from quite different sources, so that their relation to each other becomes a matter for critical debate. And Shakespeare's dramatic practice poses different critical questions when we ask—or if we ask: few do—why particular characters in a poetic drama speak only in verse or only in prose; or when we try to engage with those recent, dauntingly specialised and controversial textual studies which set out to establish the evidence for authorial revisions or joint authorship. We all read *King Lear* and *Macbeth*, but we are not all textual critics; nor are textual critics always able to show where their arguments have critical consequences which concern us all.

Just as we are not all textual critics, we are not all linguists, cultural anthropologists, psychoanalysts or New Historicists. The diversity of contemporary approaches to Shakespeare is unprecedented, enriching, bewildering. One aim of this series is to represent what is illuminating in this diversity. As the hastiest glance through the list of contributors will confirm, the series does not attempt to 're-read' Shakespeare by placing an ideological grid over the text and reporting on whatever shows through. Nor would the series' contributors always agree with each other's arguments, or premises; but each has been invited to develop a sustained critical argument which will also provide its own critical and historical context—by taking account of those issues which have perplexed or divided audiences, readers, and critics past and present.

Graham Bradshaw

Contents

Preface

This study of *The Merchant of Venice* is introductory. Its modest but not meagre aim is to guide the responses of newcomers and to freshen the thinking of those already familiar with the play in order that individual spectators and readers may form and formulate their own views about the pleasures and puzzles of *The Merchant of Venice*. This modesty is not apologetic. *The Merchant of Venice* has too often fallen victim to aggressive and single-minded interpretations. Many aspects of the play have proved contentious: its attitudes to Shylock and the Christians; the kinds of interrelations it creates between its two worlds, and its three plots; its possible endorsement of, or divergence from, Elizabethan views of Jews and usury; its status as comedy, or tragedy, or problem play; its claim to artistic coherence—all have provoked lively disagreement. In the course of this study, the many familiar critical issues are raised, but raised when and where the play itself prompts such considerations. And in following the logic of the play's unfolding, I have attempted to avoid the interpretative violence previously done to a play, the particular qualities and problems of which stem precisely from its temporal shaping. The aim is to return spectators and readers to the play and, more particularly, to the experience of the play as it unfolds scene by scene.

Any individual critical work within a series is, of necessity, an honourable compromise between the emphasis of the individual contributor and the more general requirements and structure of the series as a whole. This study follows the general outline of the *New Critical Introductions To Shakespeare* series in discussing stage history, critical reception, sources, adaptations and the larger assumptions about, and implications for, literary criticism, which any study of *The Merchant of Venice* involves. Some readers may wish to *begin* with discussion of the text of *The Merchant of Venice* and only then to proceed to considerations of larger contexts. Such readers are invited to 'begin in the middle' with Chapter 3, and will find in Chapters 3 to 7 of this book an Act-by-Act discussion of *The Merchant of Venice*.

Acknowledgements

I am indebted to the General Editor for his patience, good sense and a great deal of encouragement. I am also grateful for the time, conversations and constructive criticisms of Ruth Pitman, George Myerson and David and Sandra Hopkins. Sue Roe and her colleagues at Harvester · Wheatsheaf have proved untiringly helpful. Errors, misjudgements and infelicities are my own.

The Alexander edition of Shakespeare's work is the source for references and quotations thoughout the text. Where other works are cited, they are immediately followed by the author's surname, the date of publication and a page reference; the reader may then refer to the Bibliography for further details. Where possible, works are cited in the most easily accessible editions.

The Stage History

It is very unlikely that any single interpretation of *The Merchant of Venice* can accommodate and realise the full range of possibilities suggested in the following study. It is even less likely in the theatre. But while *The Merchant of Venice*, like all of Shakespeare's plays, easily admits of diverging theatrical interpretations, it has always challenged actors and directors to find some way of sustaining the tension which is peculiarly its own, and which makes it *both* an unsettling experience *and* an entertainment. Too often, perhaps, the theatre has failed to respond to that challenge, and has subordinated the play's dramatic substance to easier opportunities for theatrical coups, virtuoso performances and one-man shows. The most recent production by the Royal Shakespeare Company, under the direction of Bill Alexander, at Stratford in the spring of 1987, shrivelled and vulgarised the Belmont scenes and darkened Venice into a tensely homoerotic and squalid world of violent Jew-baiters. It would have been impossible not to sympathise from the start with Anthony Sher's unsentimentalised but incessantly spat upon Shylock, were one not more aware of Sher's own theatrical display than any dramatic realisation of the role he was attempting. A large part of the stage history of *The Merchant of Venice* is taken up with the repeated complaint that the actor takes precedence over characterisation, and the play as a whole. This latest production made the play all too easy for its liberal-minded audiences, although what was remarkable was the way in which some scenes went awry simply because of the vigour with which Shakespeare's words resisted the wrenching of this two-dimensional interpretation.

Such cold feet on the part of actors and directors is more than understandable in a post-holocaust world. But the tendency to fail the full substance of *The Merchant of Venice* is not limited to the theatre of the twentieth century. The temptation has always been to solve rather than realise the problem of Shylock, to present him as either the unequivocal villain or the wronged victim. In broader terms, the temptation has been to render the play as merely the romantic comedy of its Belmont lovers, or the tragedy of Shylock or, more recently, the ironic exposure of its Venetian mercenaries. But the play is all of these things— however difficult it may be to fit them together.

We know that *The Merchant of Venice* was performed at Court in February of 1605, but beyond that we have scant records of the play in Shakespeare's lifetime. Shakespeare's text was replaced on the stage in 1701 by George Granville's redaction, *The Jew of Venice*. The problematic Shylock becomes a caricature villain in Granville's version. The ways in which this simplified and static version provide an illuminating contrast to the Shakespearean original are explored in the second chapter. In 1741, Shakespeare's play was restored in the theatre with Charles Macklin offering an energetic performance as Shylock. Thereafter the play became, and has largely remained, a vehicle for the star actor. As acting styles became more elaborate in the nineteenth century, Shylock became, through the performances of Edmund Kean, Macready and Sir Henry Irving, a noble and sympathetic character of tragic status. Irving's version also exploited the potential for the other star part with Ellen Terry in the role of Portia. In the twentieth century *The Merchant of Venice* has attracted the attentions of Forbes-Robertson, Gielgud, Wolfit, Redgrave, O'Toole and Olivier, and Sybil Thorndike, Irene Worth, Peggy Ashcroft and Dorothy Tutin. Productions in the second half of this century have paid some attention to aspects of the play other than Shylock and Portia. The version at Stratford in 1953 developed the role of Antonio, and explored the relationship of Antonio and Bassanio. Jonathan Miller's production in 1970, with Olivier as a sympathetic and pained Shylock, expanded the play's interest in isolation through the figures of Antonio and Jessica, and left these two figures on stage at the end of the play, together only in their loneliness.

The Critical Reception

When we turn from the stage to the history of the play's critical reception, two further and related questions are added to those already implicit in the history of its diverging theatrical interpretations. Is the play consistent in respect of its characterisation, tone and genre? And related to this, what *kind* of creativity and what *kind* of intelligence were at work in writing the play? In 1904 A. C. Bradley answered both questions with brevity and assurance:

> One reason why the end of the *Merchant of Venice* fails to satisfy us is that Shylock is a tragic figure, and that we cannot believe in his accepting his defeat and the conditions imposed on him. This was a case where Shakespeare's imagination ran away with him, so that he drew a figure with which the destined pleasant ending would not harmonise.
>
> (Bradley 1976, p. 14)

Others have dissented both from this assessment of the play, and from the characterisation of Shakespeare's habits of mind offered here. In this study, I attempt to focus the question of coherence on the specific parts of the play which might afford us the most useful evidence in attempting to answer it. And, by placing *The Merchant of Venice* in the framework of Shakespeare's larger *oeuvre*, and by indicating some of the interrelations, echoes and anticipations to be found among the whole range of his works, I pursue an argument about the *exploratory* and *interrogative* nature of Shakespeare's creative imagination, a particular kind of imagination of which *The Merchant of Venice* is both a fine and problematic manifestation. Moreover, in the use of history and historical information to resolve the interpretative puzzles of *The Merchant of Venice*, I diverge from the tradition of historicist critics, represented in the course of my discussion of the play, who are concerned with external evidence regarding Elizabethan attitudes, and with historical and political contexts. Like them, I would deny that *The Merchant of Venice* is ahistorical or apolitical. But I argue that the play itself is the securest guide to its own historical and political complexities, and that Shakespeare's other works afford the most useful historical context for an understanding of *The Merchant of Venice*.

There is no magisterial criticism written about *The Merchant of Venice*, but there is much that is useful. It is perhaps most valuable for students of the play to acquaint themselves with a *range* of the different kinds of argument advanced about *The Merchant of Venice*. But a bald summary of the play's critical reception, detached from consideration of the play itself, is an arid and unrewarding exercise. Consequently, interested readers will glean guidance from the second chapter where the major critical issues, and examples of various writers who explore them, are placed in the context of a larger discussion about the peculiar capacity of *The Merchant of Venice* to prompt a great diversity of often contradictory responses. Thereafter I have attempted to set up debates among the critics where the play prompts such debate. Hence the critics have been gathered together over local and specific issues, but this specificity, I hope, does not misrepresent the general tenor of their various arguments and approaches. There is a double aim here: to guide the reader to critical writings which may prove helpful, but also to afford the reader numerous opportunities to test the adequacy of the critics against the play itself.

To date, the 'new' criticisms—cultural materialism, feminism, New Historicism and such like—have proved disappointing in their offerings about *The Merchant of Venice*. I have therefore decided to discuss such approaches in an Afterword—'Prejudice and Interpretation'—which addresses some of the current critical controversies and the larger theoretical issues which *any* interpretation of *The Merchant of Venice* raises.

·1·

'There are things in this comedy... that will never please'

The Merchant of Venice proves an increasingly controversial play, and it is controversial in two related ways: ethically and aesthetically. Love of various kinds, race and religion, justice and mercy, money—however bland when abstractly listed, the play's thematic concerns are perennially provocative. And, since the play's composition, history has merely conspired to accentuate that provocativeness in ugly ways. The play's attitude to its themes and their interrelations is the stuff of heated critical contention in a world ever vexed by precisely the same issues. Yet to say as much can sound portentous when we recall that this play is a comedy and an entertainment.

And this sombre characterisation of a play that offers itself as a comedy leads to the second nexus of critical controversies. Some commentators take up *The Merchant of Venice*'s own concluding references to harmony and, in their analyses, seek to demonstrate that the play is a successful realisation of its own word. For others the play is not merely unsettling: it is itself unsettled and artistically incoherent. *The Merchant of Venice* is judged to fail to sustain unity of tone, consistency of characterisation, coherence of argument and of attitude. It begins as a comedy but lurches towards tragedy with a violence which ruptures the requirements of genre, however elastic we, and

1

Shakespeare, take these to be. Others still, while recognising the same disruptions and discontinuities in the play, are less disturbed by the imputed failure of artistic coherence. Concerned more with process than product, and with the *experience* of drama, they are prepared to offer a more admiring account of the play's unsettledness. They see in *The Merchant of Venice* a felicitous coinciding of Shakespeare's exploratory imagination with one of the defining characteristics of good drama—the rich expressive potential of a sequence of actions and voices unfolding through time. The kind of intelligence which proves reluctant to subordinate interrogation and exploration to coherence is ideally suited to exploit the experiential and temporally ordered nature of the play. The particular case of *The Merchant of Venice* represents a challenge to the general tenets of criticism: from the greatest literature, in so far as we continue to value it, we ask the coherent exploration of the human condition, but perhaps *The Merchant of Venice* challenges us to value a work which reaches for discoveries and profundities beyond those which it can fully comprehend or contain. While the play may be unyielding of any adequate single interpretation, its exploratory audacity ensures that it remains a compelling comedy which entertains and unsettles by turns.

Characteristically, there is a nonchalant audacity in Shakespeare's creativity which takes risks, cultivates intensity and challenges the limits of his narratives' possibilities. His comedies are not to be transformed into tragedies, but nor are they without edge or unpleasantness. In *A Midsummer Night's Dream* Shakespeare mocks the mechanicals' anxiety over *their* play; their fear that 'There are things in this comedy of Pyramus and Thisby that will never please' (*A Midsummer Night's Dream* III.i. 8-9). *The Merchant of Venice* remains unpleasantly alive for us because it offers its audiences in dramatic form an experience common to all groupings of human beings. In the interests of the value and values of the community (and here it matters little whether we are considering nations or schoolchildren) the opposing scapegoat must be defeated and expelled, or transformed. But in the very moment of the community's triumph—on the battleground, in the courtroom, amidst the practical jokes of the playground— we glimpse a kinship with the supposed alien, and the triumph appears Pyrrhic. *The Merchant of Venice* twice renders such glimpses explicit. In the courtroom of the fourth Act heroes and villains are momentarily indistinguishable: 'Which is the merchant here, and which the Jew?' (IV.i. 169).

Secondly, as the trial proceeds, Shylock first declares Portia to be a Daniel when she appears to be prosecuting the justice of his case but now, that Daniel is transforming herself into Shylock's merciless persecutor: it is in character that Gratiano, habitually overexplicit, should make the point so unsettlingly plain:

A Daniel still say I, a second Daniel!
I thank thee, Jew, for teaching me that word.
(IV.i. 335–6)

Having come so far in our arguments, actions and commitments, that moment when black and white become grey, when opposition threatens to transform itself into identity, cannot but be unsettling and unpleasantly embarrassing. There are indeed things in the human comedy that will never please. And there are two possible critical reactions, each pursued with particular vigour and intellectual ingenuity. The first is to argue all the more vehemently for the rightness of one's initial commitments— in the case of *The Merchant of Venice*, to deny or ignore Shylock's human claims as so many of the play's own characters themselves do. The alternative is to champion the underdog—here the dog Jew—to throw one's allegiances into reverse and to vindicate the scapegoat at the cost of sentimentalising him and ignoring his faults and his threat.

While these two possible responses will be opposed in argument and in the kind of evidence they adduce, they share certain underlying characteristics. While vigorous, neither is disinterested and, while rational, both are partial. *The Merchant of Venice* may divide its audiences and critics, but it generates a shared need to argue to win, to clarify in the interests of peace of mind. Put colloquially, this comic play first asks of its audience 'How far can you go?' and then leaves us, in accounting for our responses and commitments, with the uneasy residual feeling that we shouldn't be starting from here: *The Merchant of Venice* begins *in media res* and then seems to turn back on itself. It is unsurprising, then, that the critical heritage of *The Merchant of Venice* is less the story of disinterested *descriptions* of the play and its workings than of energetic—and sometimes very odd—*reactions* to it. That is in itself testimony to the play's enduring power.

The habits of thought and emotion I've sketched above are those characteristic of prejudice; in such cases, commitment precedes the reasoning which appears to justify the commitment, and such reasoning is therefore predetermined, partial and contrary to the totality of the evidence available. One critic has remarked rather wearily that *The Merchant of Venice* is 'a theme-hunter's delight' (Leggatt 1974, p. 118): it is not my intention here to discover further themes to add to the familiar list of concerns critics have recorded in discussing the play—the conflicting loyalties of love, the antagonisms of race and religion, the debate over the means by which people gain their living, the clash between the alien individual and society, the diverging notions of what makes for value in human life. I want rather to call attention to the vital importance of the already identified themes and issues for this play and for our lives, and to describe something of the attitudes to these themes and issues which the play displays. These attitudes are characteristically prejudiced ones. Our loves and our sexuality, our race and our religion, our livelihood and the treatment we are accorded by society—such matters are fundamental in that they determine who and what we are; they define our selves. They constitute what a forlorn Antonio, at the end of the play, refers to as our 'life and living'. Prejudice thrives readily and pervasively among such fundamental matters; that goes a long way to illuminate the proliferation of themes in The Merchant of Venice and the shifting nature of its thematic focus. To emphasise one theme above the others; to insist, for example, that the play is more about usury than anti-Semitism, or more about love than justice, is to thin The Merchant of Venice and to deny one of its great insights; the conversations of the play's characters move so readily and rapidly from one issue to another because each character is so often bent on answering the prior needs of self-justification and self-vindication. It is in the nature of prejudice to display such eclecticism and lack of focus.

What follows here is not a comprehensive new interpretation of The Merchant of Venice. The play has suffered from the aggressive justifications of its champions no less than the dismissals of its detractors. It seems a rich play where the potential multiplicity of meanings is in excess of any full realisation. And to actualise any single interpretation of the play is to stress, and perhaps overstress, one of its parts at the cost of ignoring or doing violence to parts of the play developing in other, equally interesting, ways. This is an attempt to characterise, rather than resolve, the play's puzzles, and to raise questions about the limits of plausible interpretation. Such tentativeness may irritate some readers but, when the critical history of The Merchant of Venice has so often been marked by dogmatism, the play now merits a greater degree of reserve and tact.

It is implausible to insist, without qualification, on the artistic autonomy of The Merchant of Venice since the play gains enormously in intelligibility when placed in the context of Shakespeare's oeuvre as a whole. If we are to think of Shakespeare's creativity as characteristically exploratory and interrogative, and if consequently we see the greatness of a Shakespearean play not in any philosophical statement it makes but in the experience of an unfolding process of thinking which it affords, then we must concede too that in some ways *The Merchant of Venice* represents a case of the dramatist thinking very much ahead of himself. Some of our difficulty with the play arises from our sense that Shakespeare's mind is making occasional leaps well beyond what the immediate material and local context can coherently accommodate. But such incongruities are too interesting and exciting to be unquestioningly dismissed since they are manifestations of the *same* mind, of the *same* exploratory creativity as that which gives rise to the achieved design. Often in such cases a larger pressure and direction of thought again become evident, but only when we look beyond the single play to the interrelations of Shakespeare's *oeuvre*. The insights and dramatic methods of *The Merchant of Venice* bear fruit beyond the individual play.

Moreover, in emphasising the importance of process for our appreciation of Shakespeare, we need not assume an attendant progress; there is no implication intended here that, as the dramatist develops, Shakespeare necessarily gets better or more profound. In his essay on *Dante* T.S. Eliot puts the general case well, although Eliot's implicitly pejorative characterisation of Shakespeare's ignorance is for me an indication of Shakespeare's strong and dynamic intelligence, a sign of a mind not confined within any antecedently fixed system or set of assumptions:

We do not understand Shakespeare from a single reading, and certainly not from a single play. There is a relation between the various plays of Shakespeare, taken in order; and it is a work of years to venture even one individual interpretation of the pattern in Shakespeare's carpet. It is not certain that Shakespeare himself knew what it was. It is perhaps a larger pattern than Dante's, but the pattern is less distinct.   (Eliot 1951, p.245)

This notion of a developing process of literary thought is strongly suggested by the critics' often repeated sense that *The Merchant of Venice* is out of place in the chronology of the Shakespearean canon. They feel that it anticipates modes and issues treated centrally later in the *oeuvre*. The most obvious example is that of the tensions between mercy and justice exposed in Act 4. The theme was gestured at, but not explored in, the Prince's justification of Romeo's banishment in *Romeo and Juliet*: 'Mercy but murders, pardoning those that kill' (*Romeo and Juliet* III.i. 194).

The issues incubating in the early tragedy come to full life in *The Merchant of Venice* but are not contained by, nor exhausted in, the Venetian courtroom; Shakespeare repeatedly returns to them, in the formal settings of *Measure for Measure*, and in the courtroom of the mind in *King Lear* and *The Tempest*. Indeed, these later works have educated us into a kind of hindsight which increases the troublesomeness of *The Merchant of Venice*. It is not that this play fails to resolve the clashing claims of justice and mercy; it is difficult to imagine what might constitute any such resolution. But these issues erupt in the play only to be dropped with an abruptness—seen clearly in Shylock's sudden departure from the play—which suggests that the thought is ahead of itself and must be subjected to a temporary formal arrest in the interests of preserving some degree of tonal coherence. Act 5 goes on to offer us the tangential coda of the ring plot, extraordinarily open to diverging interpretations and emphases, and the play's ending proves to be a conclusion in which we are as aware of who and what are absent as we are of the characters and actions directly before us.

The Merchant of Venice undoubtedly has its limitations. Our growing sense, as the play progresses, of its complexities and puzzles derives more from a process of accretion and accumulation than from a more securely integrated development. This seems related to a certain limitation in the play's characterisation. Although our sense of these characters changes as different facets of their natures are exposed to our view, the characters—with the possible exception of Shylock—do not themselves develop. The characters' self-awareness and their insight into others are often limited. Hence many of the subversive insights into the behaviour of the Christians, into the complexities of mercy and justice, and into the conflicting loyalties of love which the play's audience registers are not available to, nor further explored by, the characters *within* the play. For this kind of more integrated exploration we must go elsewhere in Shakespeare—to the self-lacerating insights of Angelo's soliloquies in *Measure for Measure*, for example. This limitation also contributes to our sense of *The Merchant of Venice* being ahead of itself; the play repeatedly throws out teasing questions which are not then taken back into the play for more sustained development. The action of the play proceeds in ways which often appear oblivious of its own complexities, but does so with a harshly comic flagrancy which suggests that we, Shakespeare's audience, cannot but be intended to register such discrepancies. Interpretations of the play have to steer between the Scylla of potentially complacent under-readings, emphasising celebration, and the Charybdis of ingenious over-readings, emphasising irony: how far may we legitimately and fruitfully pursue the play's various puzzles?

Creativity as an exploratory process will involve anticipations and opportunities not fully realised, moments of underdevelopment and of overstretching, with all the attendant unevennesses and discrepancies. In this respect *The Merchant of Venice* is an important play in the canon precisely because it cannot be convincingly 'rescued' into any stable artistic unity, narrowly conceived. *The Merchant of Venice* is not *finished* art in either sense of the term and, fully pondered, Shakespeare can appear all the greater for that.

·2·

Responses, Sources, Contexts

The safest place to begin with so controversial a play as *The Merchant of Venice* is with effects rather than causes. In a brilliantly economical survey of the play's criticism, Norman Rabkin recently identified the essential quality of *The Merchant of Venice* to be its capacity to provoke a welter of diverging and opposing responses. Consequently Rabkin lamented the play's critical history as a series of strategies of evasion, determined either to dismiss the play, or through partiality and evasion, to coerce it into a thematic and tonal unity. Rabkin's crisp diagnosis of this critical tradition merits quotation at length:

> Such radical disagreements between obviously simplistic critics testify to a fact about their subject that ought to be the point of departure for criticism. Instead, critics both bad and good have constructed strategies to evade the problem posed by divergent responses. Some blame Shakespeare, suggesting that his confusion accounts for tension in the work and its audience. Others appeal to a narrow concept of cultural history which writes off our responses as anachronistic, unavailable to Shakespeare's contemporaries because of their attitudes towards usury or Jews or comedy. Still others suggest that, since the plays are fragile confections designed to display engaging

if implausible characters, exegetical criticism is misplaced. Though all of these strategies attract modern practitioners, they have lost ground before the dominant evasion, the reduction of the play to a theme which, when we understand it, tells us which of our responses we must suppress. The ingenious thematic critic . . . is licensed to stipulate that 'in terms of the structure of the play Shylock is a minor character' and can be ignored, or that the action is only metaphorical and does not need to be examined as if its events literally happened, or that Shylock is only a Jew, or a banker, or a usurer, or a man spiritually dead, or a commentary on London life, never a combination of these; or that *The Merchant of Venice* is built on 'four levels of existence' corresponding to Dante's divisions—'Hell (Shylock), Purgatory proper (Antonio) and the Garden of Eden (Portia-Bassanio), and Paradise'; or that the play is exclusively about love, or whatever, and, insofar as it doesn't fit the critic's formulation, it is flawed.

(Rabkin 1981, pp. 7–8)

Only very recently have critics (Leggatt 1974; Rabkin himself; Nuttall 1983; Berry 1985) been prepared to display at length a perplexity which may perhaps account for the reticence of so many of our great Shakespearean critics on the subject of *The Merchant of Venice*. The critical response to the play proves less than directly rewarding. This can be ascribed in part, as Rabkin implies, to critics' obtuseness and interpretative aggression. But it also says something more interesting about the tenacity of the play's hold on the minds of its audiences and readers. *The Merchant of Venice* proves an extraordinarily difficult play from which to free oneself into an adequate degree of objectivity, and criticism tends to be symptomatic of the play rather than illuminating of it. Indeed, such criticism can often seem a reactive prolongation of that unfolding of postures, positions and habits of mind which both characters and audience assume,

reject and reassume in the course of the play
The oddities and embarrassments which s
course of these critical arguments are co-ex
those occurring in the play and amount, in the
something of a comedy.

There are two predominating and opposed ʌys of
reading *The Merchant of Venice*. The basic division of
opinion manifests itself in a variety of ways. Thus critics
divide over Shylock. Some see in him the consistent villain
of the piece, and consequently celebrate the Christian
lovers' triumph over him. Against this, some see in Shylock
victimised humanity and, accordingly, view the play's
lovers with varying degrees of scepticism which, in extreme
cases, can amount to hostility. More particularly, there are
two focal points in such disagreements, two rich and
complex scenes where, in Act 1 Scene 3, Shylock and
Antonio first agree the terms of the bond, and, in Act 3
Scene 1, Shylock declares his intention to claim his rights in
respect of it. Critical debate, though lively, is circumscribed,
limited to discussion of character, and Shylock's character
in particular. Prior to this century, the body of criticism of
The Merchant of Venice has shown this emphasis on
Shylock, but has proved less rich or rewarding than that
which has accrued to many of Shakespeare's other plays; it
has often been occasional, prompted by particular
productions of the play and reveals, as the stage history
does, the predictable shift, as we move from the eighteenth
to the nineteenth century, in the characterisation of
Shylock—from clown and villain to the figure of wronged
humanity who merits our compassion. (See John Russell
Brown, 'The Realization of Shylock', in Brown and Harris
1961, pp. 187–210.)

When we turn from critics who discuss character to those
who discuss theme, we find the critical accounts broader,
accommodating more of the play, but the critics remain
similarly divided in their opinions and attitudes. Thus, for
some critics the play secures and celebrates valued

distinctions—between material and spiritual wealth; between venturing and usury; between generosity and possessiveness; between love and the law; between mercy and justice. For others the play works to quite the opposite effect, undermining such distinctions through dark and troubling ironies. And some such critics pursue what they see as the play's ironic mode to discover covert correspondences underlying the play's ostensible oppositions; hence, for example, the play's principal antagonists, Shylock and Antonio, are revealed to share the painful kinship of isolation and exclusion. These are larger discussions, not limited to a few of the play's great scenes, and exercised by questions of the relationship between the worlds of Belmont and Venice, and between the casket plot and the bond plot. As with considerations of character, however, the fundamental disagreement remains whether to regard the *The Merchant of Venice* as characterised by celebration or irony.

Frank Kermode is representative of those who emphasise celebration, and reveals incidentally the kind of oddity which typically accompanies the expression of such views:

> *The Merchant of Venice*, then, is 'about' judgment, redemption and mercy; the supersession in human history of the grim four thousand years of unalleviated justice by the era of love and mercy. It begins with usury and corrupt love; it ends with harmony and perfect love. And all the time it tells its audience that this is its subject; only by a determined effort to avoid the obvious can one mistake the theme of *The Merchant of Venice*.
>
> (Kermode, in Brown and Harris 1961, p.224)

The tone of this is reminiscent of that adopted by the overly brusque Antonio in his dealings with Shylock early in the play. With Kermode's earlier insistence on 'the correct interpretation' (ibid., p.222), it is all the more surprising from a critic who is later to emerge as a champion of critical pluralism, and who has always emphasised the patience of Shakespeare before his interpreters. The tension between the claimed themes of harmony and love, and the impatience and intolerance with which they are urged is odd indeed. Kermode's method of argument is also interestingly representative in the way he appeals to analogies from *nondramatic* literary modes to 'resolve' the play's difficulties and thus stabilise, and perhaps falsify, the drama; in his case the appeals are to Spenser, Milton and the Bible. Barbara K. Lewalski pursues a similar interpretation of the play, with similar no-nonsense tone and similar appeals to nondramatic modes, here biblical allusion and allegory:

> comprehension of the play's allegorical meanings leads to a recognition of its fundamental unity, discrediting the common critical view that is a hotch-potch which developed contrary to Shakespeare's conscious intention.
>
> (Lewalski 1962, p.328)

But when the importing of an allegorical framework threatens to displace rather than illuminate the particularities of incident and character, might we not wonder whether drama should be subordinated to allegory in this way? We are getting remote from the experience of *The Merchant of Venice*.

Harley Granville-Barker has proved even more brusquely untroubled by the play in his insistence that the casket plot and the bond plot have all the unreality of fairy tales, unaware in that appeal that fairy tales and folklore rarely enjoy the psychological and sociological innocence he imputes to them (Granville-Barker 1958, Vol. 1, p.335). Concerned to assimilate *The Merchant of Venice* to the pattern of festivity and merriment which he discerns in Shakespearean comedy generally, C.L.Barber finds various embarrassments in pursuing this line of interpretation;

Barber openly confesses his unease, but finds himself drawn into weak argument nevertheless:

> The whole play dramatizes the conflict between the mechanisms of wealth and the masterful, social use of it. The happy ending, which abstractly considered as an event is hard to credit, and the treatment of Shylock, which abstractly considered as justice is hard to justify, *work* as we actually watch or read the play because these events express relief and triumph in the achievement of a distinction.
>
> (Barber 1972, p. 170)

But a distinction which works only if we don't think about it, is more likely to be a distinction undermined than a distinction made.

John Russell Brown also sees *The Merchant of Venice* as a play which secures distinctions—between material wealth and love's wealth. He finds the play's own sententiousness catching, but proves less than fully responsive to the drama's dynamic testing of such static aphorisms and can be led into such contortedly protective logic as the suggestion that 'it is Shylock's fate to bring out the worst in those he tries to harm' (Brown 1962, p. 74).

Of course, all of these critics, and many others who share the same interpretative emphasis on celebration, have valuable and substantial things to say about the play, but the oddities here suggest that their readings bear a tangential relation to *The Merchant of Venice*'s essential nature.

Those critics who see *The Merchant of Venice* as an ironic play are also useful. Moreover, perhaps because they don't pursue extraneous authorities to verify their interpretations, their readings often have the advantage that they focus more attentively and sustainedly on the drama before us. Even when overingenious or wrong-headed, the particularity of their arguments seems closer to the particularities of the play itself. But is also true that these critics are often no less biased nor odd than their opponents. Both A. D. Moody and Harold C. Goddard are aware that they are not offering interpretations from first principles, as it were, but their corrective readings often prove less sure-footed than these critics might intend. Moody sees *The Merchant of Venice* as a play which 'does not celebrate the Christian virtues so much as expose their absence' (Moody 1964, p. 10), but comes repeatedly close, in his emphasising of the covert above the overt, to seeing the transparent evil of Shylock as no evil at all; Shylock's 'villainy is almost naïve and innocent' by comparison with the Christians' (ibid., p.29). At times Goddard loses his footing entirely and sinks into rhetoric and implausible metaphor:

> Even Shylock, as we have seen, had in him at least a grain of spiritual gold, of genuine Christian spirit. Only a bit of it perhaps. Seeds do not need to be big. Suppose that Portia and Antonio, following the lead of the seemingly willing Duke, had watered this tiny seed with that quality that blesses him who gives as well as him who takes, had overwhelmed Shylock with the grace of forgiveness! What then? The miracle, it is true, might not have taken place. Yet it might have.
>
> (Goddard 1960, p. 111)

If Professor Kermode sounded uncomfortably like Antonio, then Professor Goddard's pleading out-Shylocks Shylock, but without the villain's vengeance.

The Merchant of Venice's capacity to prompt these contradictory reactions has led critics to speculate about the circumstances of the play's composition and its creator's intentions. Initially, the focus of attention is the portrayal of Shylock. In H. B. Charlton's influential view, the anti-Semitic Shakespeare sets out to pander to prejudices common to himself and his audience but finds, in spite of himself, that his characteristic powers and intuitions lead to a humanised Shylock; 'His Shylock is a composite

production of Shakespeare the Jew-hater, and of
Shakespeare the dramatist' (Charlton 1949, p. 132). It is a
powerful thesis, reiterated as recently as 1980 by D. M.
Cohen, with but one alteration in its argument:

> It is as though *The Merchant Venice* is an anti-Semitic play
> written by an author who is not an anti-Semite—but an
> author who has been willing to use the cruel stereotypes
> of that ideology for mercenary and artistic purposes.
>   (Cohen 1980, p. 63)

The limitation in such arguments lies in their often
unintentionally diminishing image of Shakespeare as naïve
and inspirational, a great artist almost in spite of himself.
Shakespeare does not *stumble* on the fact of Shylock's
humanity; a writer who habitually confers inner life on the
characters he finds in his sources and who, as we shall see,
characteristically compounds the complexities of these
sources, is *cultivating* difficulty in a spirit of exploration. The
openness which allows him to make such discoveries is
matched by a resourcefulness in subduing the arising
discrepancies into some degree and some appearance, at
least, of artistic coherence.
    Most recently some critics have emphasised, in *The
Merchant of Venice*, not a failure of artistic unity but the
dynamism of drama, and have therefore shown themselves
more thoroughly admiring of the play. Ralph Berry finds it
to have 'the self-adjusting elasticity of the great play' (Berry
1985, p. 46), and finds design in the play in its temporal
shaping of the sequence of its audience's diverse responses:
the play is so organised as to *provoke* the audience's
discomfort. The boldest and most ambitious of recent
critics writing on the play locate discrepancy and
incoherence, not in Shakespeare's play, but in his, and our,
world beyond the drama, and they thus transform talk of
incoherence into praise of the play's inclusiveness.
A.D.Nuttall finds *The Merchant of Venice* characteristic of

Shakespeare's tendency 'to take an archetype or a stereotype and then work, so to speak, against it, without ever overthrowing it' (Nuttall 1983, p.124). But 'Shakespeare will not let us rest even here. The subversive counter-thesis is itself too easy. We may now begin to see that he is perhaps the least sentimental dramatist who ever lived. We begin to understand what is meant by holding the mirror up to nature' (ibid., p. 131). For Norman Rabkin, too, *The Merchant of Venice* in its inclusiveness, contradictions and complications, reflects the larger reality of a world itself unyielding of simple and single meanings. The 'artistic multivalence . . . is the mirror of an unfathomable reality which is the source of the trouble . . . a reality that cannot be cut down to a single understanding' (Rabkin 1981, p. 139–40). It misrepresents both Nuttall and Rabkin, each engaged in large considerations of Shakespeare and the nature of creativity and criticism, to adumbrate their arguments in this way and to narrow their speculations to apply only to *The Merchant of Venice*. Nevertheless, *tout comprendre c'est tout pardonner*, and we might worry that their emphasis on Shakespeare's reality and nature is at the cost of criticism *and* appreciation of his art, and that the play continues to trouble despite the grandeur of such exonerations: *The Merchant of Venice* perhaps represents a moment of integrity too questioning and insufficiently artful to contain multifarious truths within the coherence and consolation of art. Some, at least, of the irreconcilable elements in *The Merchant of Venice* are not shaped into telling insight, but remain unrewarding flaws, symptomatic of lines of thought discarded in the course of the exploratory process. Indeed, Nuttall's and Rabkin's arguments are not too far removed from the greater stringency of Dr Johnson who celebrates Shakespeare as the poet of nature whose incoherences and discrepancies, though natural, are incoherences and discrepancies none the less.

Like *King Lear*, *The Merchant of Venice*'s provocativeness

goes beyond critical response to creative redaction.
Famously, *King Lear* spawned Nahum Tate's corrective
Restoration work, *The History of King Lear*, and more
recently, Edward Bond's *Lear*. *The Merchant of Venice*
follows a very similar pattern, giving rise to George
Granville's *The Jew of Venice*, first performed in 1701 and
dominating the stage until Macklin's return to the
Shakespearean text in 1741; and, more recently, to *The
Merchant*, by Arnold Wesker, himself Jewish. What is
interesting in the case of both works, given my argument for
the inherently problematic *and* dramatic nature of
Shakespeare's play, is how both redactions, though in
opposing ways, simplify and clarify the issues of the original
by means which also substantially reduce the *dramatic*
power of the results. Granville's play secures Shylock as
comic villain and celebrates love and friendship in the
figures of Antonio, Bassanio and Portia. The most relevant
omission is that of the critically contentious Act 3 Scene 1 of
Shakespeare's play, where we had seen Shylock's reaction
both to the loss of his daughter and to Antonio's losses;
Shylock's villainy becomes much less ambiguous as a result
of that omission. The now clear contrast between Shylock
and the Christians is repeatedly and crudely pointed up in
such moments as Shylock's aside in the scene, merely
reported in Shakespeare but now dramatised by Granville,
of Bassanio's and Antonio's pained parting:

> *Bassanio* . . . Oh my Antonio! 'tis hard, tho' for a
> Moment,
> To lose the Sight of what we Love.
> *Shylock (aside)*   These two Christian Fools put me in
> mind
> Of my Money: just so loath am I to part
> with that.
> (Spencer edn, 1965, p.372)

In Granville's version, the original play's sententiousness

is heavily augmented, playing, as it does, into the Restoration's shrivelled sense of dramatic action as merely subservient to, and illustrative of moral statement. Granville reverses the characteristic Shakespearean process of creation to the extent that the drama is now contained by its moral sententiae, its 'good Morals and just Thought' as the play's Epilogue puts it (ibid., p. 401). Action once exploratory is now ornamental, and the resulting play is both stable and static. The dramatic urgency of the early scenes in Shakespeare's play is supplanted by an interpolated scene of stylised moralising in which Antonio, Bassanio and Shylock drink to Friendship, Love and Money, respectively, and this moralised tableau-like quality is further enhanced by the addition of a masque reiterating the values of Love and Friendship.

As a creative response to what he sees as Shakespeare's anti-Semitic play, Arnold Wesker's *The Merchant*, first performed in Stockholm in 1976, is altogether more extreme—and understandably so, given the racial identity of the playwright and the holocaust after which he writes. But the integrity of his intention is destructive of the dramatic qualities of his play, and it is unsurprising that *The Merchant* failed in New York and has never been performed in London.

In Wesker's version, the casket plot is but the foolish philosophical whim of Portia's father, and the love of Portia and Bassanio is marked, not by any romantic idealism, but by pragmatism and realism. Jessica runs off with the 'sort of' poet, Lorenzo, in similarly mundane fashion, although she later proves stouter and more articulate in Shylock's defence than Shakespeare's Jessica did. The shallowness of the young Venetians is much emphasised. Wesker's Shylock and Antonio are old friends in their mid-sixties. This Shylock dominates his play: he is tyrannically hospitable; he is a miser only in so far as he hides Hebrew books to prevent the Christians burning them, and only his daughter is treasured above these books; a committed feminist, Shylock is out to demonstrate in the education of Jessica that daughters can be the intellectual rivals of sons. Money-lending is never Shylock's full-time occupation, and he uses his wealth to function as a one-man Arts Council in the Venetian ghetto, financing art, music, literature, philosophy and architecture. His wealth is further used in helping the poor and the Jewish refugees fleeing the Inquisition. Moreover, the Jews, through taxes and forced 'loans', are shown to be one of Venice's principal sources of finance.

Wesker's Shylock and Antonio agree their bond reluctantly, only because the law demands it. And it is a merry nonsensical bond indeed, in mockery of the law and agreed over much mutual tickling. Later Shylock's sole reason for not abandoning the legal claims he has in respect of the lapsed bond is that others in the Jewish ghetto fear— and have cause to fear—that the Christians will use such a precedent against them in future dealings. Shylock must stick to the law to ensure the law's future protection of his people, and his reaction when Portia deploys her legal tricks is thus a relieved 'Thank God'. Shylock pays the price of seeming to threaten the life of a Christian, and now contemplates a departure for the Holy Land.

But Wesker's corrective urge is repeatedly of a vehemence and urgency in excess of what the immediate dramatic contexts he creates will sustain, and the emphatic extremity of his message is thus intelligibile only if we look beyond the particular moments in which it is delivered to the Shakespearean play against which it is a reaction. Wesker's *The Merchant* has a problematic status as a work of art and is not the autonomous drama it ostensibly appears but is parasitic on the play it reviles. The characters' voices are subordinated to the single, wilful voice of the playwright pursuing his argument with Shakespeare.

For us here, Wesker's redaction illuminates the Shakespearean original in two ways. In transforming his sources, Shakespeare had rendered Shylock a more complex and sympathetic character than the villain in the various tales he used, and clearly Wesker is moving very much further in the same direction. But in one important way Wesker is reversing the effect which Shakespeare had on his source materials. Wesker returns the story to its earlier simplicity, and unravels the teasings and testings which Shakespeare's creative amalgamation of a variety of sources had produced. The result is stridently univocal and undramatic. The three centres of narrative interest— Shylock and Antonio, Portia and Bassanio, Lorenzo and Jessica—are now securely and hierarchically ordered with the Shylockian tale almost eclipsing the other two. And the questions and challenges arising from the Shakespearean interplay of narratives are thus suppressed. Wesker renders the casket test cynical so that the Portia we see there is no longer at odds with the quick-witted character we see in the trial scene. Bassanio becomes once again the godson of the Antonio figure of Shakespeare's primary source, Ser Giovanni's *Il Pecorone*, and Antonio ages accordingly; the further amatory tension which the love of Antonio for Bassanio had introduced into Shakespeare's play is again excised in Wesker's version. The story, now so favourable to the Venetian Jews, has in other respects come full circle and Wesker is at odds with Shakespeare not merely in attitude but in method and art. While more obviously liberal, Wesker is also less exploratory.

Wesker's play vindicates his Jew. But it is a neat irony that Wesker's play is more akin to the flatter simplicities of Shakespeare's sources than to *The Merchant of Venice* itself; the story can become comforting for the prejudiced and the enlightened alike only if its Shakespearean truths are simplified.

The possible sources of *The Merchant of Venice* are multiple and various, admit of varying degrees of probability and influence, and extend both very far back to longstanding traditions of folklore, and to near-contemporary plays, some of which are now lost. (The full facts are discussed by Geoffrey Bullough [1957], Kenneth Muir [1977], and John Russell Brown in the Arden edition of the play[1961].) What is salient is the audacity implicit in Shakespeare's combining of such diverse material, his cultivation of the problematic and the probing. Shakespeare is going out of his way to make things difficult for himself and his audiences. In Ser Giovanni's *Il Pecorone*, the impecunious Giannetto is dependent on his Venetian godfather, Ansaldo, to finance the amatory pursuit of a widowed lady of Belmonte, whose devised test is altogether more basically sexual and mercenary. To win her, the suitor must bed her—not an easy task, since she habitually knocks him out, prior to bedtime, with some doped wine. If the suitor fails, he forfeits all his wealth. Effectively, the lady of Belmonte is running an enterprising business. Giannetto's third attempt on the lady is again financed by Ansaldo, despite the godfather's having been bankrupted by Giannetto's two previous ventures. Ansaldo now borrows from a Jew and is dependent on a bond which, if he fails to keep it, demands the payment of a pound of his flesh. The lady's maid warns Giannetto off the wine, Giannetto successfully performs the required test—the narrative spares us any details of the lady's initial surprise but reassures us that finally she is highly delighted by his performance—and Giannetto takes charge of Belmonte. Eventually, he recalls Ansaldo's bond and realises that his godfather's life must be in danger. Giannetto returns to Venice to be followed there by his lady in disguise, and she successfully performs her tricks in the Venetian courtroom. The ring intrigue follows but is quickly cleared up in Belmonte, where godfather Ansaldo is cheerfully married off to the lady's maid.

Borrowing from other sources, Shakespeare multiplies both his cast-list and the story's complications. Thus the Jessica story is the synthesis of elements and hints from a wide range of narratives: she owes something to Abigail, the daughter of Barabas, Marlowe's *Jew of Malta*; she echoes the daughter of the usurer in Munday's *Zelauto*, a story which, with its financial borrowings and cruel bonds, influences *The Merchant of Venice* in multiple ways; and Jessica derives, too, from *Il Novellino* of Masuccio, where a young girl plunders her miser father to run off with the youth who is his debtor. The important point here is that in *The Merchant of Venice* Shakespeare seems to be multiplying his young couples and to be producing a number of triangular relationships which mingle obligations and loyalties of love and money (father—daughter—lover, friend—suitor—lady). By such means he sets up testing analogies among the various centres of dramatic interest. In what ways are the relationships between, first, Jessica and Shylock and, second, Portia and her father, similar? How does Bassanio differ from Lorenzo? Do Portia's and Bassanio's attitudes to money differ substantially from those of Lorenzo and Jessica? To this end, too, Shakespeare alters the relationship in *Il Pecorone* between Ansaldo the godfather and Giannetto the godson, to the loving friendship of Bassanio and Antonio. And Shakespeare rejuvenates the Ansaldo figure to further that emphasis. The neatness of Ser Giovanni's original is intentionally disrupted as Gratiano now marries the lady's maid, Nerissa, and in Shakespeare's asymmetrical ending, Antonio is left in disquieting isolation. A new complicating relationship comes into play in Shakespeare's drama. In contrast, Wesker, as we have seen, firmly subordinates the various love stories to the story of Shylock, and restores Antonio to his former dignified and disinterested age.

The Jew and/or usurer who is to become Shylock in *The Merchant of Venice* is frustrated in courtrooms as diverse as those of *Il Pecorone*, *The Ballad of Gernutus* and Munday's *Zelauto*, but Shylock's antecedents are not further punished. The new emphasis on the trial of Shylock and its painful consequences for him is Shakespearean; it deepens the seriousness of the threatening villain and invites speculation about the inner condition of Shylock's future life and about the society that preserves itself by such harsh means. Characteristically, Wesker again mitigates the isolated silence of Shylock's exit from the Shakespearean play in the new image of his projected pilgrimage to Jerusalem.

But perhaps the largest change which Shakespeare makes is in the borrowing of material from the Christian allegory of *Gesta Romanorum*, which allows Ser Giovanni's test of virility and seduction to be displaced by the decorous formality of the casket test. The trickery of the trial scene and the sexual trickery in Belmonte in *Il Pecorone* are all of a piece. They belong to a coarser and simpler comic world, fabliau-like in its ribaldry. When Shakespeare imports the casket plot into his play, this bawdry gets pushed to the side of the drama and is expressed through the figures of Gratiano and Nerissa. Bassanio's wooing of Portia is conducted by way of the caskets and involves the elevated and stylised presentation of rich depths of human feeling. Fabliau-like tales concentrate on the entertaining intrigues of action, while what we might describe as the romantic elements in the narrative of *The Merchant of Venice* invite its audiences and readers to look beyond events to matters of morality, feeling and human worth. It is this curious mixture of kinds of story which produces the greatest interpretative puzzles of *The Merchant of Venice* and may afford some explanation of the play's capacity to prompt opposing responses.

Shakespeare's fusion of this variety of sources is not without flaw; Bassanio, for example, is introduced as Antonio's 'most noble kinsman', a residual detail left over from *Il Pecorone*, but this relationship is never again mentioned in the play. But Shakespeare's bringing together of the realism of *Il Pecorone* and the romantic qualities from *Gesta Romanorum* produces the distinctive challenge of *The Merchant of Venice*: the shifting nature of the literary worlds in which the various stories are played out; the uncertainties over the kinds of response appropriate to the play's various characters; and the typical tensions between the play's characters and the situations in which they find themselves. Is Bassanio out of place in the elevated world of Belmont's moral testings? Is Portia more suited to being the dignified lady of Belmont or the quick-thinking manoeuvrer in Venice? In which scene and in which world are Portia and Bassanio most truly themselves?

Again in contrast, Wesker in his version refuses to enter imaginatively into the expressive life of the casket plot convention and views it externally, as it were, as merely the mad whim of a foolish philosopher, a whim to be circumvented by some devious thought in order that a shallower and more tawdry love between Wesker's Portia and Bassanio can come to fruition.

Wesker's *The Merchant* illuminates the controversies which surround *The Merchant of Venice* in a second way. Throughout his play, Wesker is much exercised by the problem of interpretation and repeatedly off-loads undigested and undramatic lectures on Jewish history on the slender and insufficient pretext that Shylock, who gives voice to them, is a garrulous hoarder of books, much interested in his racial past. In attempting to locate some stability of attitude among the ambiguities of *The Merchant of Venice*, and to constrain the play's troublesome meanings, literary critics often appeal beyond literature to history and historical contexts. Although few literary historians would defend the assumption in the abstract, they often argue, in their considerations of *The Merchant of Venice*, *as if*, unlike literature, history were straightforwardly factual, unambiguous and not itself in need of interpretation. But *within* Wesker's play, historical information is extensively used as an honourable, if dramatically clogging, means to further Wesker's polemical argument and vindicate the Venetian Jews. Wesker's example usefully reminds us that historical argument, like art, is never merely factual and is rarely disinterested.

Arguing that Shylock is a villain, that Shakespeare and his audiences were, to a man, prejudiced against Jews, and that the practice of usury was universally reviled, though practised none the less, E.E.Stoll is representative in his naïve confidence in Shakespeare's 'thoroughly Elizabethan taste', 'the popular imagination', 'the established traditions' and so on. Stoll exhibits, too, a tendency to argue from origins, and in doing so, to argue *The Merchant of Venice* back to the cruder simplicities of its antecedents. Thus Shylock is dragged back to the Jews of medieval iconography and the Mystery plays, and to the Barabas of Marlowe's cruder, more farcical *Jew of Malta*—though, as Stoll doesn't note, the Christians in that play are not shown much more favourably than Barabas himself. But, even allowing that Stoll's characterisation of the times is predominantly accurate, *The Merchant of Venice* may be a response to, as well as a reflection of, popular beliefs and prejudices (Stoll 1927, pp. 255–336).

One particularly neat example of history's untidiness, its tendency to complicate rather than clarify, lies in Renaissance England's attitudes to usury, an issue central to our play. But even that is not strictly true. Rather oddly, critical interpretation of *The Merchant of Venice* so often circles around the issue of usury when, in fact, no transaction involving usury occurs in the dramatic action of the play. (See, for example, E.C.Pettet, '*The Merchant of Venice* and the Problem of Usury', in Wilders 1969, pp. 100–13.) Shylock is by profession an usurer, although we never see him behaving as one on stage, and none of the numerous financial dealings and misdealings in the play involve usury. Yet characters within the play judge, or prejudge, Shylock by his profession rather than by his immediate actions, and critics beyond the play—especially those who see Shylock as the villain of the piece but wish to defend the play from accusations of anti-Semitism— maintain that emphasis. This phenomenon is but one of the play's examples of the workings of prejudice and its infectiousness: judgements are formed on the evidence of, or hearsay about, the past, and such judgemental habits preclude the possibility of innocence in the present and particular. Yet it remains true that Shylock is an usurer and that usury is important to the play, even if that importance has been exaggerated. History proves less helpful than it might, and, like the play, displays an ambiguous and equivocal attitude to usury.

In 1571 English law legalised usury, despite the evidence that it was ruining the more profligate among the landed gentry caught out by the inflation attendant on the rise of commerce. In 1572 Thomas Wilson published his *Discourse Upon Usury* which reiterates, energetically and at length, medieval and religious hostility to the practice of usury. And this is a text much favoured by purveyors of Elizabethan World Pictures, despite, it seems, Elizabethan practice. But in the third edition of his *Essays*, published in 1625, Francis Bacon, writing 'Of Usury', takes a more sanguine and balanced view. He argues that, given human frailty, usury is a necessity and discovers not merely the disadvantages but the benefits of the practice. Between Wilson and Bacon comes *The Merchant of Venice*, written at some time between 1596 and 1598. It would seem that in their actions, in their discursive writings, and, indeed, in their plays, these Elizabethans do not take an unequivocally black view of usury.

In this example I am gesturing briefly at the intellectual and social history of Renaissance England. But *which* history are we to appeal to? If we are seeking the security of a context for *The Merchant of Venice* then geography conspires with history to augment our difficulties. Do we look to Shakespeare's England? Or to the history of Venice? Or, more problematically still, to the history of Belmont? Are we not rather dealing with a coalescing of various kinds of history and fiction which occurs within the dramatist's mind and which we are more likely to recover from an examination of the play, than from history books? And if we look beyond Shakespeare to the history of his audience, we might wonder whether Shakespeare plays *to* his audience's assumptions, or plays *against* them or, most likely, does both in his usual complex way.

Nevertheless, *The Merchant of Venice* is not ahistorical. Indeed, it is itself an historical document which *contains* history's complexities and ambiguities—although the play is not *merely* that. But *The Merchant of Venice* isn't autonomous either, and if we need a context for the play, then what follows here suggests that Shakespeare's larger *oeuvre* answers most fully to that need. Of the same historical period, created by the same mind, and in the same literary mode, Shakespeare's other plays illuminate *The Merchant of Venice* but do violence neither to its individuality nor its complexity.

·3·
Beginning in the Middle

We readily recall the first scene of, for example, *Macbeth* as an inspired and memorable beginning—not least because that opening's violence of setting, characters and language, is so immediately striking. The first scene of *The Merchant of Venice* is rarely singled out in such a way because, while it has its richly comic moments, it appears unobtrusively casual. Alexander Leggatt shrewdly remarks on the 'detailed humanity' of the characters in this play and finds in their speeches 'a naturalism of manner' involving 'the revelation of feeling beneath apparent small talk' (Leggatt 1974, p. 119). Much of the opening scene seems a comedy of small talk. It treads very lightly in respect of issues and attitudes, and it seems to me to run counter to the scene's fineness for the pens of critics, underlining 'significant' lines, to render it otherwise. Love, friendship, money and religion are much mixed up with each other in this first scene and it is precisely the scene's success that *if* we notice any consequent muddles of values—and we well may *not*—then we are not disturbed by them. Of course, some audiences and some readers will have strong political and theological principles and therefore will balk, honourably and legitimately, at *any* entanglement of love, money and religion. But their argument is with much larger things than the opening conversations of *The Merchant of Venice* and, indeed, later

29

events in the play itself will furnish much more substantial
material for such argument.

With hindsight we can see larger issues looming, but the
opening of this play eases us into its vivacious world and
only later does the full impact of the play's action catch up
with us and, perhaps, catch us out. Here we see the meetings
of friends, friends not without problems and friends in
varying states of happiness and unhappiness, but there is
nothing in *The Merchant of Venice's* opening scene like that
explosive antagonism between father and daughter which
erupts at the beginning of *A Midsummer Night's Dream*.
Here, for example, we are not troubled that Salerio, in the
enthusiasm of his supposings, gets his theology and his
commerce mixed up in the course of a comically ill-
conceived attempt to cheer up Antonio:

> Should I go to church
> And see the holy edifice of stone,
> And not bethink me straight of dangerous rocks,
> Which, touching but my gentle vessel's side,
> Would scatter all her spices on the stream,
> Enrobe the roaring waters with my silks,
> And, in a word, but even now worth this,
> And now worth nothing?
>   (I.i. 29–36)

The merchants of Venice clearly deal in luxury items, but
the lyricism of Salerio's evocation ensures that we are more
likely to be attracted by the rich exoticism of the
merchandise itself than by any opportunity to moralise
about indulgent hedonism. The world of this play is an
opulent one, and if that opulence is precarious and a source
of ennui in some of the characters' lives, it does not yet
trouble us. After all, the starving masses are not much in
evidence in this world where, as we later see, even the
clown's father, old Gobbo, can muster a basket of doves by
way of a present.

If the Venetian concern with commerce does not trouble
us, nor does the Venetian style of courtship. In the
obliqueness of his approach to Antonio for yet further
funding of these amorous adventures in pursuit of Portia,
Bassanio is clearly embarrassed, but again that
embarrassment is to Bassanio's credit, part of his
recognisable and detailed humanity. This charmingly
ordinary hero is in pursuit of a girl rich in spiritual value,
rich in physical beauty, and just rich:

> In Belmont is a lady richly left,
> And she is fair and, fairer than that word,
> Of wondrous virtues.

> (I.i. 161–3)

Bassanio is a fortunate man in finding that love and money
go so neatly together, but we have no reason to doubt that it
is love none the less; there aren't enough saintly, poverty-
striken plain Janes to go round and someone has to marry
the Portias of this world.

What I have said above overstates the case, but it is
important to emphasise just how agreeably ordinary and
'worldly' this world of the play's opening proves to be; it
invites us to recognise the familiar with pleasure, or more
accurately perhaps, it invites us to enjoy the exotic made
familiar by the easy, familiar exchanges between friends. It is
important also to stress the extent of our necessary
ignorance of these characters and their circumstances at the
play's opening; to import information from later in the play
here, would be to distort the initial impression. The play, in
its opening scenes, invites a generously appreciative
response and anything judgemental, moralistic or, indeed,
idealistic seems inappropriate.

It is as if Shakespeare is establishing the form and terms of
his play's concerns before the issues themselves emerge with
identifiable substance. We can see something of this in the
case of Antonio in the opening scene: here the source of

Antonio's sadness is yet obscure and we have no knowledge against which to measure the rightness of the various opinions which characters offer about it. The middle which begins *The Merchant of Venice* is the middle of a conversation which introduces us to the comedy of an exasperated and exasperating Antonio, the melancholy merchant. An emphatic outburst reveals Antonio half-desirous to be relieved of these companions. Yet his vehemence ensures him a brief, uninterrupted silence in which to indulge that moment of curiously public self-communing which, in turn, will afford his companions further material for the exercise of their opulent and, for us, entertaining loquacity. And thereby, too, whether intentional or not, Antonio assures himself of their further attentions:

> In sooth, I know not why I am so sad.
> It wearies me; you say it wearies you;
> But how I caught it, found it, or came by it,
> What stuff 'tis made of, whereof it is born,
> I am to learn;
> And such a want-wit sadness makes of me
> That I have much ado to know myself.
>
> (I.i. 1–7)

Many more urgent and anxious questions will be asked about knowing who and what we are before this play is over. At this moment these friends are not good for each other in the way that friends often aren't. Antonio *is* unhappy, but he is also being difficult, and enjoying being difficult. He remains resentfully tight-lipped while Salerio and Solanio, ostensibly to be helpful, outdo each other in guessing games as to the source of Antonio's sadness. Comically, their vividly poetical elaborations—if they don't hit the mark—may only give Antonio more things to be unhappy about: his ships, his investments, foul weather, dangerous rocks. A part of the melancholy and withdrawn Antonio is yet attentive to and enjoying of this. He is happy to take the opportunity to display his judiciousness as a merchant whose 'ventures are not in one bottom trusted', and he is ambiguously and over-vehemently responsive to Solanio's after-thought that Antonio is in love. All three *know* that this has not been the merriest of meetings and, in parting, convey obliquely, again as friends often do, their mutual affection: Salerio and Solanio refer apologetically to the appearance of 'better company' and 'worthier friends', while Antonio reassures them that he does not take their departure amiss.

The arrival of Gratiano, Lorenzo and Bassanio gives Antonio another opportunity to wonder aloud—and provocatively—about who and what he is. In turn this proves too good an opportunity for the Dutch uncle in Gratiano to miss:

> *Antonio* I hold the world but as the world,
>   Gratiano—
>   A stage, where every man must play a part,
>   And mine a sad one.
> *Gratiano*   Let me play the fool.
>   With mirth and laughter let old wrinkles
>   come;
>   And let my liver rather heat with wine
>   Than my heart cool with mortifying groans.
>   Why should a man whose blood is warm
>   within
>   Sit like his grandsire cut in alabaster,
>   Sleep when he wakes, and creep into the
>   jaundice
>   By being peevish?
>   (I.i. 77–86)

Critics are unanimously and understandably dismissive of Gratiano as frivolous and insensitive; he belongs at the coarser extremity of this world. It is usual for them to follow Bassanio here in dismissing Gratiano's lecture to Antonio as 'an infinite deal of nothing'. (We might recognise, however, that Bassanio is far from disinterested and is giving Antonio the assessment which Antonio wants to hear.) A.D. Moody is representative here. He presses the subversive implications of the shallowness of Gratiano, Bassanio's friend, for our estimate of Bassanio and the Venetians generally. Thus, in the course of this critique Moody berates the 'grotesque preaching' of Gratiano's advice to Antonio in this first scene (Moody 1964, pp.22–3). Yet in 1817 Hazlitt, while not dissenting from the general assessment of Gratiano, was responsive in his own way to a moment of uncharacteristic seriousness and sensitivity. Gratiano 'is the jester of the piece. Yet one speech of his, in his own defence, contains a whole volume of wisdom' (Hazlitt 1955, p.216). Gratiano fears, though without the insensitivity usually imputed to him, that the unsociable Antonio might nevertheless have an eye to the world's respect and opinion, and that Antonio's curt disclaimers may be a covertly insinuating means of establishing a social identity; proclaimed isolation may be a form of social indulgence. Gratiano's speech is a serious defence of levity and, in making it, Gratiano is at parenthetic pains to be seen as a friend with no intention of giving offence:

> I tell thee what, Antonio—
> I love thee, and 'tis my love that speaks— . . .
>
> (I.i. 86–7)

He is at pains, too, not to overplay his hand, fearing that his directness may destroy Antonio's sympathy and render his advice ineffectual: 'I'll tell thee more of this another time' (I.i. 100). What is interesting in this initial exchange between Antonio and Gratiano is the radically different attitudes to who and what they are that this pair's elaboration of the familiar trope—'all the world's a stage'—throws up: Antonio's notion of his self is deterministic and single— 'every man *must* play *a* part'; Gratiano's free and protean—

'*Let* me *play* the fool'. We simply don't know enough as yet to establish which character is right here, although we shall not be surprised if there is an element of truth on both sides. The lightness of the introductory touch is remarkable.

These moments, easily glossed over initially, when the individual questions his identity and defines himself among and against the group, will multiply in number and increase in urgency and substance as the play progresses. A whole series of related questions exfoliate as a consequence of this accumulation of repeated moments. Is the individual excluded or self-excluding? Are such individuals defining themselves negatively against their society and in terms of absences and lacks, or are they insisting on distinctive qualities which are a source of genuine pride and strength? Do those others who, like Gratiano and later Jessica, refuse to fix themselves in any single role in favour of a protean 'playfulness', show an agreeably accommodating sociability or a want of integrity? Is the refusal to join the group, to play society's games on society's terms, the product of a genuine and individual scrupulousness or is it a covert form of attention-seeking, a way of attracting society's eye and admiration? In the first scene of the play such questions are focused on the figure of Antonio; as the play proceeds, these questions will be raised in respect of a diversity of characters in diverse circumstances. But, even in the greater urgency and seriousness of the play's later moments—when, for example, Shylock demands 'hath not a Jew eyes?'— Shakespeare has no clear and unequivocal answers to give: this exploratory drama works to leave such questions open and, perhaps, unanswerable.

This exploration of the self and sociability in *The Merchant of Venice* is a typical example of the turns of Shakespeare's economic yet fecund imagination whereby, in this case, a strand of thought which runs through *Romeo and Juliet* re-emerges here so transformed that the continuity is not immediately recognisable. In that play Romeo isolates himself in the assumed role of lover of

Rosaline only to be returned to his full self and a full sociability through the enabling power of his love of Juliet. Mercutio's delighted exclamations thus afford one substantial commentary on the issues which are to be reworked so thoroughly in *The Merchant of Venice*: 'Now art thou sociable, now art thou Romeo; now art thou what thou art, by art as well as by nature . . .' (*Romeo and Juliet* II.iv. 85–7). *The Merchant of Venice* renders Mercutio's confidence in such a formulation problematic and puzzles over the ways in which one can and cannot be both sociable and oneself.

Plays often begin *in medias res*, and we have seen how *The Merchant of Venice* begins in the middle of what one infers to have been a lengthy and unfruitful conversation. But in fact the play begins in the middle of larger things and in larger ways than that. The world and action of this play are burdened by their past to an extraordinary degree. Gradually the audience is explicitly informed, and often invited to make inferences, about that past. Thus it is often *in retrospect* that the play's actions and characters prove more troubling than might initially appear.

Bassanio's relationship with Antonio is compromised by Bassanio's previous borrowings: already overdrawn, he needs to call yet again on the reserves of friendship in order to pay the original financial debt. In Portia's pursuit of love, 'the will of a living daughter [is] curb'd by the will of a dead father'. Antonio's dealings with Shylock are uncomfortably coloured by a series of previous encounters. Portia and Bassanio are not meeting for the first time in this play. Similarly, in the case of Lorenzo and Jessica, we infer that some substantial, if clandestine, courting has preceded the play's opening. Shylock's relationships with Jessica and Lancelot Gobbo are weighed down by the accumulated treatment of past years, and, more generally, Shylock is burdened not merely with the past experiences of his individual life, but with the past of his racial ancestors. Even in the case of the minor characters, such as Morocco, we see something of the ways in which past actions and treatment have shaped present character and behaviour. We shall see, in the third scene of the play, how *locally* Shylock's immediately prior behaviour makes any straightforward acceptance of his offer of friendship impossible: the larger contexts which past actions in this world have generated function similarly and more pervasively. The innocence and freedom of new beginnings are not available to the characters of *The Merchant of Venice*. Moreover, the play is so shaped that something of this experience of beginning in the middle transfers itself to the audience's experience of the play: we make assumptions and commitments which are later to be challenged or unmade in uncomfortable ways. This manipulation of the chronology of his story seems part of what Ralph Berry, writing of the 'discomfort' of *The Merchant of Venice*, notes as the dramatist's unsettling tendency 'to build into the text a strategy for confronting the audience with its own assumptions and wishes' (Berry 1985, p.46).

But the focus of the second scene continues to emphasise the agreeable tip of a potentially disagreeable iceberg. The first scene introduced the Venetian world, the second introduces Belmont. It is common to remark generally on the difference between these two locations but what, in fact, is initially striking is their similarity. The two representatives of Belmont—Portia and Nerissa—seem the same kind of people, speaking the same kind of language and concerned with the same kind of things as the Venetians. If there is a disjunction, it is between Bassanio's preceding poetic description of Portia and the prosaic reality of a Portia who mingles something of Salerio's prolixity with her wit and who, like Antonio, is 'aweary of this great world'. Portia seems more humanly suited to Bassanio than the idealism of his own words recognises. If Portia's character as it is introduced here is somewhat at odds with the more high-flown elements of Bassanio's description and with conventional notions of the romantic heroine, then Portia's attractiveness gains rather than suffers, just as in *Much Ado About Nothing* Beatrice proves more vivaciously sympathetic than the more conventional Hero. The lives of Portia and Nerissa have an individuality which is not to be parcelled up in any neat aphorism, as their ensuing dialogue demonstrates. 'Good sentences, and well pronounc'd' is Portia's appeasing concession to Nerissa's good-humoured remonstration and, challenged to follow such nuggets of moral wisdom, Portia elaborates on the resistance of human life to such sententious containment. And Portia goes on to mock Nerissa's admiration of 'good sentences' in a flow of imaginative wit which is itself richly sententious: Portia deploys adage and aphorism against themselves and, while she concedes human weakness, she also implicitly insists on an openness to experience, an individuality and flexibility which are not to be contained in, nor simplified by succinct and sententious commonplaces:

> If to do were as easy as to know what were good to do, chapels had been churches, and poor men's cottages princes' palaces. It is a good divine that follows his own instructions; I can easier teach twenty what were good to be done than to be one of the twenty to follow mine own teaching. The brain may devise laws for the blood, but a hot temper leaps o'er a cold decree; such a hare is madness the youth, to skip o'er the meshes of good counsel the cripple.
>
> (I.ii. 10–22)

Here the play raises one aspect of its own *modus operandi*— the tensions which the play repeatedly sets up between maxims and aphorisms and the particularities of the dramatic action which seem both to illustrate and to subvert such maxims and aphorisms. D. J. Palmer remarks that *The Merchant of Venice* is 'the most sententious of all the comedies before the problem plays' (Bradbury and Palmer 1972, p.97). Examples are not far to seek: 'It is a good divine that follows his own instructions'; 'The devil can cite Scripture for his purpose'; 'All that glisters is not gold'; 'The quality of mercy is not strain'd'; 'Nothing is good . . . without respect'. *In themselves* many of these sayings—often marked by negatives—prove less than immediately lucid. When we consider the *application* of such sayings to the events in the play, our interpretative puzzles multiply. In *Romeo and Juliet* Shakespeare had come somewhat unstuck with the authority figure of the Friar, whose sententiae and aphorisms seem intended as a straightforward commentary on the play's actions. The Friar's sayings and truisms, however, seem paltry in relation to the magnitude of that action and, unintentionally perhaps, the Friar emerges as a small-minded and morally dubious figure. The univocal morality associated with sententiousness seems at odds with the powers characteristic of the dramatist. Sententious elements in *The Merchant of Venice* serve a much more complex role within the play's overall dramatic pattern.

'Sententiousness' is perhaps too pejorative in its modern connotations and is too limiting a description for the presence within *The Merchant of Venice* of a great number of literary elements, extending beyond individual sentences, adages and aphorisms to the various plots, especially the casket plot, the various trials and testings, and to various objects with great potential for symbolic resonance— caskets, rings, bonds. All of these, in other literary contexts, might serve as a means to articulate straightforward moral lessons and wise commonplaces. In such contexts—one thinks of the simpler kinds of fables and allegories, for example—the particularity and individuality of action and character are subordinate to the exemplification of generalities and truisms. *The Merchant of Venice* reverses that emphasis so that the play's action is not contained by its sententiae; instead, these are not merely illustrated but tried and tested, by the particularity of the dramatic action. The relation between moral generalities and the specifics of dramatic action thus becomes a problem for interpretation.

D. J. Palmer describes the effect as one in which 'our attention is often held by moral arguments of one kind or another, while a different order of awareness and response is being solicited by other dramatic means' (Bradbury and Palmer 1972, p.98).

Seeing or reading *The Merchant of Venice* takes on some of the qualities we associate with the experience of looking at a photographic double exposure. Criticism should not be too ready to resolve that image. Yet critics favourable to the Christians and hostile to Shylock tend to resolve the play in terms of its own aphorisms and adages, to underplay the discordant particularities of the play's action, and to catch something of the play's own sententiousness. The opposing reading, attentive to the discrepant details of the action, is itself too ready to offer neat ironic reversals of such overtly stated aphorisms and moral lessons: Harold C. Goddard is representatively, and too easily, clever in announcing that 'Portia is the golden casket' (Goddard 1960, p.112). Words enjoy no such straightforwardly direct nor inverted relation to the world of *The Merchant of Venice*.

In this scene Portia's witty play of *sententiae* is a distraction from, rather than a solution to, her more immediate and pressing problem: the *terms* of the casket test, while disagreeable to Portia, are less immediately troubling than the more practical inconvenience that news of the test has brought so many crowding to Belmont. Bound by the terms of her father's will, she finds herself besieged by suitors. And Belmont does indeed appear to have become the congregating place for international folly to a degree that would strain the hospitality of the best of hostesses. Perhaps, in contrast to Shakespeare's original audience, some of us are currently so sensitive to racialism that *any* racial joke is disagreeable and remains so, in spite of any larger qualifying context which the drama might create. Such a position is more than understandable, but it is rather sombre and it does involve a loss, a loss of the moments of comedy here and also of the questions about racial attitudes which *The Merchant of Venice* itself will strive to raise in its audiences' minds. Portia's and Nerissa's cataloguing of Portia's suitors represents Shakespeare's talented exploitation of one of the stock devices of comedy, the racial joke, and their exchanges can appear funny and innocently enjoyable. The joke is particularly rich when it is against the audience itself, as in the case of the young baron of England, richly arrayed in international motley but ill-suited to anything other than plain English conversation:

> You know I say nothing to him, for he understands not me, nor I him: he hath neither Latin, French, nor Italian, and you will come into the court and swear that I have a poor pennyworth in the English. He is a proper man's picture; but, alas, who can converse with a dumbshow? How oddly he is suited! I think he bought his doublet in Italy, his round hose in France, his bonnet in Germany, and his behaviour everywhere.
>
> (I.ii. 60–8)

The joke is richer still when it is against the audience's next racial neighbour, the pugnacious Scottish lord. (References to his Scottishness are removed from the Folio text of 1623, long after the Scottish James has come to the throne. The Union deprives the joke of some of its topicality, and its removal is presumably a consequence of the understandable assumption that royalty is more quick than most of us to be unamused.)

Portia's and Nerissa's idle chatter appears innocent in part because they are more concerned to characterise men's follies than their vices, and because the racial stereotypes are described in a dance of verbal inventiveness which modern comedians rarely match. But the apparent innocence is also a consequence of absence: as yet such suitors are firmly off-stage and no particular individual is before us to challenge, and to suffer under, the stereotyping description and thereby complicate our responses to the comedy.

Shakespeare is ever ready to exploit the temporally ordered nature of the play, and the particularly dynamic, changing and challenging experience which a play affords its audience as a consequence of the fact that events and insights are altered and complicated as the play unfolds through time. In the later play, *Measure for Measure*, he will allow the fully controlled and gradual encroachment of the particular case of Claudio and Juliet to complicate our rational and emotional responses to the general and abstract debate about mercy and justice which that play conducts. *The Merchant of Venice* anticipates this dramatic method and, in the play's complicating exploration of racial attitudes, makes similar use of the expressive and interrogative potential of a sequence of scenes, events and arguments unfolding progressively before the audience. As the play proceeds, Morocco and Shylock both appear on stage as particular human beings who jostle disconcertingly against the initial prejudices and stereotyping labels. It is more particularly in their later appearances that the fool in Morocco and the villain in Shylock give way to a fuller revelation of human suffering. Here, early in the play, Portia's witty quip, continuous in style with the scene it concludes, anticipates the arrival of Morocco and the exposure of more complicated meanings for that word 'complexion' than Portia, for all her verbal dexterity, appears to recognise: 'if he have the condition of a saint and the complexion of a devil, I had rather he should shrive me than wive me' (I.ii. 116–18). But, in fact, we don't have to wait for Morocco's entrance for this testing of racial stereotypes and prejudices to begin.

The arrival of Shylock in the third scene of the play reverses the pattern of the previous scenes: amity turns to hostility; free-flowing conversation to stilted resentment and recalcitrant pedantry; the lively reciprocity of wordplay to laboured puns, cultivated miscomprehensions and unheeding tirades. In the first scene Bassanio was the reluctant asker and Antonio the eager giver. Bassanio is now in the opposite position before a ponderously recalcitrant Shylock, who is yet only too ready to seize any hurriedly unthinking remark from Bassanio as an excuse for tangential obfuscation. Shylock labours his joke about land-rats and water-rats and pirates (pi-rats), but he is also quick to take offence at an invitation to dinner:

> Yes, to smell pork, to eat of the habitation which your prophet, the Nazarite, conjured the devil into! I will buy with you, sell with you, talk with you, walk with you, and so following; but I will not eat with you, drink with you, nor pray with you.
>
> (I.iii. 28–34)

In the immediate context it is Shylock who is wilfully excluding himself from company and conviviality and from any meeting of minds. But what weight of previously suffered exclusions and rebuffs may be determining this present preservation of aloofness and display of resentful anger? Antonio's arrival ensures that Shylock withdraws further into himself: neither greets nor affects to recognise the other and a little comedy ensues, alternating oblique conversation conducted through the intermediary Bassanio with exaggerated and deliberately belated courtesies.

What makes Shylock the most interesting and strongest character Shakespeare has created in this play is his greater capacity for self-insight. Shylock knows more truths about himself than the others know of their own natures, and he is prepared to tell them and to use them. Mistreatment has nurtured a resentful consciousness, and that resentment is quick to show itself in Shylock's first long speech in the play:

> How like a fawning publican he [Antonio] looks!
> I hate him for he is a Christian;
> But more for that in low simplicity
> He lends out money gratis, and brings down

The rate of usance here with us in Venice.
If I can catch him once upon the hip,
I will feed fat the ancient grudge I bear him.
He hates our sacred nation; and he rails,
Even there where merchants most do congregate,
On me, my bargains, and my well-won thrift,
Which he calls interest. Cursed by my tribe
If I forgive him!

(I.iii. 36–47)

Critics are sent off on a wild goose chase by this revealing aside in attempting to settle the play's theme as that of race, or religion, or money. The point of Shylock's speech is quite the opposite. Does Shylock's resentment have its origins in differences of religion? Or race? Or the conduct of financial dealings? Is Shylock's antipathy based on general considerations or does it relate, more narrowly and specifically, to Antonio's mistreatment of Shylock personally? Is Shylock's resentment a consequence of Antonio's mistreatment of him? Or does the greater hurt lie in the *public* nature of Antonio's abuse? And where does Shylock feel this public hurt the more? His pride? Or his purse? The reason for Shylock's hatred of Antonio is never brought to a stable focus because it is in the nature of prejudice for such 'reasons' to slip and slide uglily over an antecedently conceived hatred. And here Shylock veers, too, between feelings of resentful inferiority and assertions of superior pride; a sense of inadequacy alternates with contempt. The Iago-like improvisations and 'reasoning' suggest a compulsive and destructive resentment lurking in Shylock.

But if we sense that Shylock, as he is introduced in this play, is malevolent, then we see too that Antonio is indeed in a false position. Antonio's vulnerability as a petitioner produces, by way of a self-protective reaction in him, an overly brusque assault on the point at issue—the need to borrow Shylock's money. For once, Shylock has very much the upper hand and will come anywhere other than to the point. Recurring throughout the play is a pattern of repetitions which alternates between moments where a character asserts his own identity—often in ways we may feel to both self-vindicating and self-imprisoning—and, in contrast to these, moments where a character challenges the consistency and integrity of others. The latter first appear in Portia's general and good-humoured observation that 'It is a good divine that follows his own instructions', and in her sketch of Monsieur Le Bon as 'every man in no man'. Now the challenge has a more specific and serious target: when does a willingness to accommodate to circumstances, to 'break a custom', become a failure of principle and loss of dignity?

> but hear you,
> Methoughts you said you neither lend nor borrow
> Upon advantage.

(I.iii. 63–5)

What matters to the play about Shylock's consequent digression into the story of Jacob and his uncle Laban's sheep, from the Old Testament—Antonio's and Shylock's *common* heritage—is that its interpretation is problematic. Shylock here is as intent on scoring racial and religious points as he is concérned about usury. Whether Jacob's somewhat odd form of genetic engineering is or is not analogous to usury, is much debated by the critics, as the notes in the Arden edition abundantly demonstrate (John Russell Brown 1961, pp.25–7). Like the play's problematic *sententiae*, such parables have the potential for multiple applications, and their interest lies in the way they may be interpretatively appropriated to serve the needs of the individual character at the individual moment. They form part of a rhetorical strategy of self-assertion and self-justification. Antonio's commentary on Shylock's theology declares as much and, in their sententiousness, Antonio's

words have of course the potential to turn back on Antonio
himself and on the Christians generally:

> Mark you this, Bassanio,
> The devil can cite Scripture for his purpose.
> An evil soul producing holy witness
> Is like a villain with a smiling cheek,
> A goodly apple rotten at the heart.
> O, what a goodly outside falsehood hath!
>
> (I.iii. 92–7)

At the point of crisis in *Measure for Measure* Angelo will
deepen Antonio's devilish insight into a moment of
glaringly harsh self-discovery, and the subversive revelation
will be exposed and explored at the centre of that play:

> O place, O form,
> How often dost thou with thy case, thy habit,
> Wrench awe from fools, and tie the wiser souls
> To thy false seeming! Blood, thou art blood.
> Let's write 'good angel' on the devil's horn,
> 'Tis not the devil's crest.
>
> (*Measure for Measure* II.iv. 12–17)

But we are concerned with a moment early in *The Merchant
of Venice* and remote from the sexual heatedness of *Measure
for Measure*. In our play, with the possible exception of
Shylock, characters prove more limited in their self-
awareness and in their awareness of human weakness and
hypocrisy: the ironic subversions which tell against the
play's Christians, form an underlying sequence of
interrelated hints largely unrecognised by the characters but
more troubling for the audience. This ironic subtext offers
another way of accounting for Ralph Berry's description of
the 'discomfort' of an audience watching *The Merchant of
Venice*. (Berry 1985, p. 46). In what ways are we to enjoy a
play in which we sense a growing gap between our own

perception of the action and the characters' sense of what they are doing and what is happening to them? How do we cope with a villain who, never less than villainous, yet seems increasingly to have the greater truths on his side? Antonio's and Shylock's theological debate over usury is not resolved in the play itself but peters out in Antonio's frustration as Shylock pursues a new and less oblique tack:

> Signior Antonio, many a time and oft
> In the Rialto you have rated me
> About my moneys and my usances;
> Still have I borne it with a patient shrug,
> For suff'rance is the badge of all our tribe;
> You call me misbeliever, cut-throat dog,
> And spit upon my Jewish gaberdine,
> And all for use of that which is mine own.
>
> (I.iii. 101–8)

It is both shocking and supremely right that Antonio should be revealed as the greatest anti-Semite of them all. Here Harold C. Goddard remarks that 'Antonio abhors Shylock because he catches his own reflection in his face' (Goddard 1960, p. 88). The play will gradually reveal Antonio's sadness to have its source in the exclusivenesss of his love for Bassanio, an affection reciprocated but not in the same degree and not exclusively so. But we would make Shakespeare too much our contemporary if we were to invoke the term 'homosexual', since that modern description displaces the emphasis from the love we see on stage, reducing it to matters of sexual inclination. Moreover, the Renaissance manages a more open and unprejudiced acceptance of such chaste male love than we can perhaps muster: Solanio's and Salerio's commentaries on Antonio's feelings for Bassanio record nothing other than admiration. Nevertheless, Graham Midgley and W. H. Auden are right to call attention to Antonio as an outsider, isolated emotionally as is Shylock racially (Wilders 1969, pp. 193–207, 224–40). And Shakespeare's disinterestedness ensures a more inclusive portrayal of this lonely figure than the emphasis on 'nobility' and 'pathos' of some critical accounts (Moody 1964, p. 24). Antonio's love for Bassanio is too true to be altogether good. Antonio's desire to display the extremity of his selflessness in public is not without a degree of egotistical manipulation. He shares with Shylock—'Hath not a Jew eyes?'—a talent for the victim's blackmailing and self-advertising whine. The letter of request he will later send Bassanio is written in such a bleating manner as to be impossible to deny: 'all debts are clear'd between you and I, if I might but see you at my death. Notwithstanding, use your pleasure, if your love do not persuade you to come, let not my letter' (III.ii. 320–3). And Antonio prays, not precisely to see Bassanio before he dies, although that is what he intends, but more revealingly, for Bassanio to come to *witness* his death:

> pray God Bassanio come
> To see me pay his debt, and then I care not.
>   (III.iii. 35–6)

Antonio may well *feel* himself to be the 'tainted wether of the flock' but he is *not* the man to say it in a public display of self-pity. In part, he is forging a social identity for himself out of self-abnegation, 'thriving on rejection' (Berry 1972, p. 129).

To emphasize the darker side of Antonio's love is to distort the larger impression, in the play as a whole, of the rightness of his generosity and the selflessness of his sacrifice. But it does illuminate the local uglinesses, as in Antonio's vehement outbursts of hostility towards the Jew, and exposes the covert kinship of Antonio and Shylock. Antonio's mistreatment of Shylock constitutes the dramatic embodiment of one of the play's profound insights into the complicating workings of prejudice; sadly the tendency of human nature is to treat others not as we would be treated but as we *have been* treated. The vulnerable make the best victimisers and, if we do learn from experience, we are more likely to learn to re-enact rather than reform its pains: intolerance generates further intolerance. Those characters who seemed initially to be warmly and ordinarily human are gradually showing themselves to be all too human.

In this comedy of ill-according manners, neither Shylock at his most seemingly generous, nor Antonio at his most seemingly grateful, can recognise and meet the other as a full human being. Each must wrest events into an interpretation couched in terms which minister to his own comfort and self-esteem. An aggressively matter-of-fact and business-like Antonio cannot conceal from Shylock what is, for the Jew, a rare opportunity to exercise social power, and thus Shylock tauntingly imposes on the situation an interpretation which exposes the reality of Antonio's vulnerably hypocritical position. Shylock, the masterly manipulator of morality, seeks to control *both* sides of the conversation:

> Well then, it now appears you need my help;
> Go to, then; you come to me, and you say
> 'Shylock, we would have moneys'. You say so—
> You that did void your rheum upon my beard
> And foot me as you spurn a stranger cur
> Over your threshold; moneys is your suit.
> What should I say to you? . . .
>
> (I.iii. 109–15)

Shylock proceeds to caricature the act of generosity which Antonio seeks from him. This can only provoke a tirade from Antonio which is ruthlessly met by Shylock's too long withheld offer of friendship and kindness. And this, in turn, leaves Antonio no alternative but the silence of exasperation and embarrassment.

> Why, look you, how you storm!
> I would be friends with you, and have your love,

Forget the shames that you have stain'd me with,
Supply your presents wants, and take no doit
Of usance for my moneys, and you'll not hear me.
This is kind I offer.

(I.iii. 132–7)

Like so many words in this play, 'kind' is multiply ambiguous—generous, recognising of our common humanity, tit for tat—and Shylock's apparent openness has a cynical edge.

The merry bond agreed, Antonio in turn can only express his gratitude by translating Shylock back into his own gentile terms. The linguistic somersaults in which Antonio is involved here betray the stubborn fixity of his habitual assumptions and prejudices, prejudices which remain all too secure in spite of the particular Jew now leaving the stage. Not for the last time in the play, certain names perform uncomfortable double service, referring both to the stereotype and to a particular human being:

Hie thee, gentle [gentile] Jew.
The Hebrew will turn Christian: he grows kind.

(I.iii.172–3)

At the end of this scene, the series of Shylockian manoeuvres culminates in the agreement of the merry bond and, while our perspective continues to have much in common with that of Antonio and Bassanio, we now have cause to worry *with* them and *about* them. Critics, such as H. B. Charlton and Harold C. Goddard, who are more sustainedly sympathetic to Shylock, protest the initial innocence of Shylock's proposed bond. They offer a very different and, for me, implausible reading of Shylock's introductory scene, often in tones not too far removed from Shylock's own, of misunderstood hurt and self-vindication. But to infer reasons for Shylock's behaviour which make it comprehensible, is not to make it any less disagreeable.

However, Charlton and Goddard do have one substantial point to make, and one worth stressing:

> Even with the signed bond and its forfeiture clause in his possession, Shylock's chances of demanding the forfeit are in fact almost equal to the chances of a first prize through the holding of one ticket in the Irish Sweepstake. A Shylock diabolically bent on ensnaring an enemy for whose blood he lusted might surely have shown sufficient ingenuity to scheme for shorter odds.
>
> (Charlton 1949, p.147)

> the idea that as intelligent a man as Shylock could have deliberately counted on the bankruptcy of as rich a man as Antonio, with argosies on seven seas, is preposterous.
>   The bond . . . does indeed reveal a hidden desire on Shylock's part to tear out Antonio's heart, but that is a power-fantasy pure and simple. It is like a child's 'I'll kill you!' Such things are at the opposite pole from deliberate plans for murder, even judicial murder.
>
> (Goddard 1960, pp.92–3)

Only Richard III and the villains in detective novels have masterplans. In Shylock's case, the telling comparison is with the villain in *Othello*. While both Iago and Shylock are malevolent, and while each is possessed by a hatred of Othello, and of the Christians respectively, neither has a large worked-out plan to bring down their enemies. The difference between the two characters lies in the fact that while, at the beginning of *Othello*, we encounter Iago already actively engaged in making mischief for Othello, Shylock's malevolence is only gradually coerced into action by the events of the play. Even less than Iago, who improvises precariously from moment to moment with whatever chance offers him, does Shylock have preconceived intentions and plans. And, unlike Iago, Shylock in the course of the play is to be given further, more obvious and immediate causes for acting on resentment and ill-will—his daughter's betrayal and the Christians' subsequent taunts. Only then does Shylock's evil take on that specific directedness which characterises Iago throughout *Othello*. Here Shylock's mutterings represent a disposition rather than a scheme:

> If I can catch him once upon the hip,
> I will feed fat the ancient grudge I bear him.
>
> (I.iii. 41–2)

But the disposition is malevolent, none the less, and Shylock's offered bond remains an act of perversity calculated to embarrass rather than an act of generosity designed to appease.

By the end of Act 1 we have seen two characters bound by formal bonds and bonds which, in each case, extend in their consequences beyond the single individual: Antonio is to be bound to Shylock, and Portia to the terms of her father's will. And the latter contract, despite its romantic aura, is no less harshly legalistic than the former. But the play is threaded through with a great number of less formal bonds, obligations and connections: familial bonds, bonds of friendship, of love, of race, of religion and of the past. The word 'bond' and its variants echo throughout *The Merchant of Venice* and the play may be regarded as an extended exploration of its ambiguities. Bonds are what hold human society together and give human life meaning and dignity. But an overly narrow insistence on the terms and obligations of a bond, an insistence on keeping one's word, an insistence on the letter, can devalue and dehumanise. Links can become manacles. As with the individual character, so with the transactions and relations which bind such individuals into a larger society, we again encounter in *The Merchant of Venice* that tension between principle and accommodation. What are the limits of humane behaviour?

·4·
Complicating Matters

Act 2 complicates matters considerably. There are a large number of comparatively short scenes, a variety of characters and a proliferation of issues in this Act. In purely formal terms, these are managed in a superb way which typifies Shakespeare's mastery of stagecraft: the urgencies of the various departures from Venice and the urgencies of the various choosings in Belmont are interwoven with a seemingly effortless ease which enhances the suspense of the action in each location. But we might also say that there is too much here, an almost excessive rush of imaginative energy. It is perhaps in this part of the play that we most feel the limitations implicit in Alexander Leggatt's comment on *The Merchant of Venice* that 'an unusual number of characters . . . appear prominently for a scene or two, and are then forgotten' (Leggatt 1974, p. 121). Here characters are somewhat underwritten, and the mutually illuminating potential of the various centres of action remains potential rather than fully actualised, so that we must beware of academic over-reading in the fleshing-out of latent relatednesses. This is very much the defect of a virtue; Shakespeare's creative energy seems here to be such that he does not linger in substantiating any *one* strand of thought. Thus, especially when we compare *The Merchant of Venice* with other Shakespearean plays, we can see some opportunities not fully taken. One example we recognise when we think of *As You Like It* and *Twelfth Night* is the potentially complicating androgyny of the female characters' disguise. Jessica's male garb in this Act, and Portia's very different but similarly masculine costume in the later trial scene allow each character 'a masculine freedom of action' (Leggatt 1974, p. 137), and thus underline the passivity which habitually characterises the female role in both Venice and Belmont. But such insights do not work themselves to the centre of the various romantic plots in the play and remain incidental: Jessica feels a degree of unease in her boy's costume in this Act, and Portia's disguise later allows for the initiation of the ring plot. But *The Merchant of Venice* sustains none of the complications which run throughout *As You Like It* and *Twelfth Night* as a result of Rosalind's and Viola's respective transformations. There is the sense that Shakespeare's insightful exploitation of one of the given conditions in the theatres of his day is being glimpsed here but is as yet incubating.

It is typical of *The Merchant of Venice* that, as Act 2 begins, Morocco is introduced at the moment of wondering about who he is and how he is seen by others: 'Mislike me not for my complexion' (II.i. 1). Portia *does*, as her earlier quip had made clear: 'if he have the condition of a saint and the complexion of a devil, I had rather he should shrive me than wive me' (I.ii. 116–18). Now the individual character is on stage to interrogate the adequacy of her attitude. The word 'complexion' encloses the appearances of Morocco in the play, for it is Portia's words of concern about his colour which first introduce him, and he is to leave the stage at Portia's final aside regarding his character:

A gentle riddance. Draw the curtains, go.
Let all of his complexion choose me so.

(II.vii. 78–9)

'Complexion' was more richly meaningful for the Elizabethan audience. Its senses moved through what we commonly recognise by the word today—colour of the skin—to the idea of 'complexion' as the combination of humours, physical qualities which affect character, and beyond that sense to the word's most inward and psychological meaning—the condition of the mind, temperament and character. The scenes involving Morocoo are a dramatic exploration of that richness of meaning, and Portia, perceiving only the external sense of the word, remains unchallenged by its more inward meanings. That is a mark of shallowness in Portia; with the hindsight of our knowledge of Shakespeare's later works we can measure Portia's limitations in contrast to Desdemona's deeper appreciation of *her* Moor when that heroine audaciously disregards mere appearance and emphatically declares, 'I saw Othello's visage in his mind' (*Othello* I.iii. 252). Portia's caricaturing banter in the previous Act appears less straightforwardly enjoyable in retrospect, less innocent, more unthinking.

Yet we should not misrepresent the balance of these scenes and overemphasise the degree to which the Morocco episode tells against Portia. We mislike Morocco because he is a fool, a fool whom we would certainly not wish on the heroine. Portia's conduct in these scenes is demure, if cold. And we enjoy the covèrt expression of her characteristic wit in the joke at Morocco's expense—an empty compliment, fair sounding but in fact saying nothing:

> But, if my father had not scanted me,
> And hedg'd me by his wit to yield myself
> His wife who wins me by that means I told you,
> Yourself, renowned Prince, then stood as fair
> As any comer I have look'd on yet
> For my affection.
>
> (II.i. 17–22)

Only at the end of Morocco's second appearance do we
glimpse his present pain and the aridity of his future life. But
even that inwardness is distanced from us since his
departing words take the form of a conventional rhyming
farewell:

> Cold indeed, and labour lost,
> Then farewell, heat, and welcome, frost.
> Portia, adieu! I have too griev'd a heart
> To take a tedious leave; thus losers part.
>
> (II.vii. 74–7)

It is, moreover, a pain which, despite her limitations, Portia
too half-catches and registers in her '*gentle* riddance'.

In their exchanges Morocco's foolish limitations loom
larger than Portia's. Although we should not underestimate
Morocco's alien appearance to a racially inexperienced
Elizabethan audience, we mislike Morocco for reasons quite
other than his colour. And one of them is Morocco's
obsessive and exclusive assumption that the sole ground for
misliking him *is* his colour. Of course, we infer that
Morocco raises that issue to dismiss and deny it because
past experience has taught him that if he does not raise it
himself, others will. Portia has already furnished evidence
of that, albeit not in Morocco's presence. The victim of
prejudice often defines himself against, and thus indirectly
derives his identity from, that very prejudice. We also
mislike Morocco for the reasons he adduces in refutation of
such prejudice. His boasts of physical courage, his talk of
blood-letting and blood-comparing, his swearing by his
scimitar, his off-loading of previous battle triumphs—such
feats might impress in the worlds of Tamburlaine or
Macbeth. But here the alliterative and hyperbolic bombast
conveys a self-absorption which renders Morocco oblivious
to the cushioned Belmont society in which he now finds
himself. Like Shylock and Antonio, Morocco has suffered
from being at odds with his world—and we can regret that—

but, again like them, he too thrives on and by that fact, and we mislike him for it. Ironically, Morocco's external complexion *has* been allowed to shape the inner complexion of his character: the manacles forged by social prejudice have been internalised by Morocco's own mind. The play's wit and psychological insightfulness combine in the inevitability of Morocco's choice of casket. His grandiloquent pondering is entirely confined to considerations of appearance. He is unable to resist the equation of outward form and inner worth which leads him to a golden choice. His mind is so formed as to be incapable of working at any other level.

The Prince of Arragon, the second of Portia's suitors whom we see in this Act, clearly does not fire Shakespeare's imagination in the way that Morocco did. His role in the play, significantly confined to a single brief appearance, is more narrowly functional. His trial allows a further elaboration of the nature and terms of the casket test and, in his grandeur, he provides further testimony that Portia is much sought after, and worth the seeking. His role extends little further than a meditation on the caskets, and the play offers few other clues to his character. Pride and a dislike of vulgarity seem to combine to produce an inconsistently argued choice of casket. Thus Arragon rejects the lead casket because of its base appearance, but then refuses to align himself with thé 'barbarous multitudes' who 'choose by show', and consequently dismisses the gold. Arragon's choice of the silver casket is justified by a lament that the world no longer manifests a congruence between men's inner worth and their social and financial status. Such a lament, in other circumstances and given a more substantial treatment, would not sound amiss in, for example, a Jonsonian play. Here, however, Arragon's often-repeated and egotistical insistence on the 'true seed' of 'clear honour' might seem to hint faintly at a future Shakespearean character also comically contorted by his obsession with honour—the Hotspur of *I Henry IV*. For somewhat

muddled reasons, then—and the muddle seems as much
Shakespeare's as it is Arragon's—Arragon decides to
'assume desert', and the silver casket presents him with a
fool's head and a decidedly opaque account of why Arragon
has got it wrong:

> The fire seven times tried this;
> Seven times tried that judgment is
> That did never choose amiss.
> Some there be that shadows kiss,
> Some have but a shadow's bliss.
> There be fools alive iwis
> Silver'd o'er, and so was this.
> Take what wife you will to bed,
> I will ever be your head.
> So be gone; you are sped.
>
> (II.ix. 63–72)

Arragon's character is underwritten; we just do not see
enough of him to know *what* he is worth and *what* he
deserves.

I feel that the shallow and improvised quality here reflects
as much on the dramatist as it does on the character. Asked
why Arragon fails the test, I feel on securer ground if,
instead of attempting analysis of character and moral
argument, I shift the terms of the question and suggest that
he fails because he has the misfortune to be only the second
in a line of three characters who are to make the choice of
caskets before us. Shakespeare is not particularly interested
in Arragon's moralisings and homilies, and this seems the
negative aspect of the play's general tendency to grow
beyond the casket plot's sententiousness into the more
ethically complex area of particularised and embodied
human actions. The play is not subordinated to the
coherent working out of the moral lesson of the caskets but
makes very effective opportunistic and, at times, ironic use
of its homiletic and sententious material. In this brief scene,

however, that material seems somewhat inert: it is left to the creative interpolations of director and actor in individual productions to flesh out Arragon and determine, more emphatically, how we are to interpret his appearance. Indeed, it is at the end of the scene in the announcement of Bassanio's impending arrival that both verse and characters show themselves most dramatically alive.

This scene with Arragon gives rise to one further small but quite typical difficulty. In all probability it may be no more than a local slip, consequent on what I have suggested is the slackness of the scene as a whole. But our attention may be drawn to it because, at the beginning of this short scene, Arragon rehearses the terms of the test, terms which include the solemn and extreme undertaking that

> if I fail
> Of the right casket, never in my life
> To woo a maid in way of marriage . . .
>
> (II.ix. 11–13)

Yet, only some fifty or so lines later, the casket itself delivers the reply: 'Take what wife you will to bed . . .' (II.ix. 70). Is this, as Dr Johnson supposed, an example of Shakespeare's forgetfulness, or is the discrepancy intended to be noted as a sarcastic cruelty? And the more we look here, the more our difficulties multiply, almost to the point of silliness: is this a release from the original terms of test; need 'what wife you will' necessarily be your *own* wife? Here again is a small example where the play's imperfections are not easily disentangled from its ironies and ambiguities. If Shakespeare is nodding, then the error seems nevertheless of a piece with the larger ambiguities of the play. If the darker implications are intended, then the intention is not here sufficiently realised. And locally the audience is shielded from the pain of any intended insult because Arragon's farewell is couched in the caskets' own jingles, remote from the inwardness which blank verse can convey:

Still more fool I shall appear
By the time I linger here.
With one fool's head I came to woo,
But I go away with two.
Sweet, adieu! I'll keep my oath,
Patiently to bear my wroth.

(II.ix. 73–8)

Objectively regarded—especially in the light of the
particularised humanity of the play's central characters—
the casket test may seem by this stage nonsensically
primitive, adrift from the characters who play it out. But we
should not underestimate the potency and pleasure of such
stylised theatricality for an audience, even if some kinds of
literary criticism have proved less than appreciative in
describing and explaining it. These casket scenes hold and
excite audiences in the theatre in ways which academic
criticism easily underestimates. Moreover, the play's most
odd and powerful mingling of realistic character and stylised
convention—Bassanio's choice—is yet to come.

Interwoven with the formalities of the various choosings
and departures in Belmont are a profusion of less formal
choosings and departures in Venice. Without the
stylisation of Belmont, the similar concern with the
interrelation of love and money shows itself more blatant in
Venice.

The Venetian focus in this Act is on Jessica, but the events
centred on her are ushered in by some comic business from
the play's clown. Launcelot Gobbo takes his leave of
Shylock and 'buys' himself a new master and a new identity
in the form of the fool's more guarded livery. H. B.
Charlton dismisses Gobbo as 'the slenderest and most
pointlessly fatuous of Shakespeare's clowns' (Charlton
1949, p. 128), while Joan Rees regards his scenes as 'filling'
material: 'Launcelot Gobbo has no necessary function in
any of the stories, and neither has his father' (Rees 1978,
pp. 20–1). Certainly, the comedy of the scenes involving

Gobbo, when contrasted with other aspects of the play, is cruder, less inward and more reliant on stock devices, but in these respects it is also in character with the less sophisticated people around whom it plays. Moreover, this kind of comedy may be more narrowly confined by its historical moment: Launcelot's confusions are amusing only when we readily recognise them as such, and many of his lines have now become obscurities in need of editorial annotation.

But Gobbo does have a role in the larger patternings of the play. First, he serves as a device to illuminate further the character of Shylock in the emphasised contrast between Shylock and Bassanio as the clown's two very different masters. As Jessica's companion in conversation. Gobbo provides a further perspective on Jessica since, like her, he transfers allegiance from one group to another. Moreover, in this Act, Launcelot's various doings function, in a precisely detailed way, as a parodic anticipation of Jessica's actions. The way in which the comic simplicity of Launcelot's antics precedes and sharpens our appreciation of Jessica's behaviour is typical of the play's characteristic pattern—as seen in Portia's comedy of racial prejudice—of presenting to the audience a series of actions, situations and attitudes in a straightforwardly comic way only to represent the same actions, situations and attitudes in more complex and ambiguous form. The play deepens and complicates our responses as it unfolds through time. It is one thing for Shylock's servant to cast the Jew as 'the very devil incarnation' in his burlesque psychomachia; it is quite another when Jessica, Shylock's daughter, has come to regard her father's house as 'hell'. It is robustly funny when Launcelot deceives his father momentarily with *the idea that* he has lost his son, 'the very staff of [his] age, [his] very prop'; it is altogether more serious and consequential when Jessica is brought to deceive her father, and Shylock is left to react to the knowledge that his daughter is indeed forever lost to him. It is easy for Launcelot to change his allegiances, his role and his clothes; such transformations prove much more difficult for Jessica.

The Shylock who oppresses both Launcelot and Jessica in these scenes is largely distanced from us as a comic grotesque: it is the play's strength that when Shylock is more centrally before us, we should see him as *both* more seriously evil *and* more humanly vulnerable. But, as we see him here, he is very much the stage Jew, summed up in his portentous dream of money-bags. Launcelot's and Jessica's language of hell and devilry is, in its context, the overstatements and exaggerations of characters whose witty spirit is far removed from Shylock's literalism: Launcelot may be 'famish'd in his service', but the clown is not wasting away; Jessica may live in 'hell', but it is a hell whose principal pain is 'tediousness', and a hell hitherto populated by a 'merry devil' in shape of Launcelot Gobbo. Shylock is characterised here by his tight opposition to masques, music and merriment (see Barber 1972, p. 165) and by bustling and pedantic officiousness:

> Well, Jessica, go in;
> Perhaps I will return immediately.
> Do as I bid you, shut doors after you.
> Fast bind, fast find—
> A proverb never stale in thrifty mind.
>
> (II.v. 50–4)

His schemes for revenge on the Christians extend no further than their larders:

> I am bid forth to supper, Jessica;
> There are my keys. But wherefore should I go?
> I am not bid for love; they flatter me;
> But yet I'll go in hate, to feed upon
> The prodigal Christian.
>
> (II.v. 11–15)

Similarly, the 'huge feeder', Launcelot Gobbo, is parted

with—somewhat regretfully—but in the hope that he may help Bassanio 'to waste/His borrowed purse'.

This distancing is maintained when, subsequent to Jessica's elopement, we hear for the first time of Shylock's reaction to the loss of a daughter. We are told of it rather than shown it, and told in terms of bawdy and satirical comedy. (Even here, however, we are not entirely accepting of Solanio's account of the matter. In drama we have an eye to the speaker as well as listening to what is being said: overhearing a joke is different from being told one. And when the joke is as cheaply overplayed as is this one, we are learning something not merely about Shylock's moral and emotional confusions but also about the shallowness of Solanio and Salerio.)

> I never heard a passion so confus'd,
> So strange, outrageous, and so variable,
> As the dog Jew did utter in the streets.
> 'My daughter! O my ducats! O my daughter!
> Fled with a Christian! O my Christian ducats!
> Justice! the law! My ducats and my daughter!
> A sealed bag, two sealed bags of ducats,
> Of double ducats, stol'n from me by my daughter!
> And jewels—two stones, two rich and precious stones,
> Stol'n by my daughter! Justice! Find the girl;
> She hath the stones upon her and the ducats.'
>
> (II.viii. 12–22)

Shylock is seen here as a figure for the malicious fun of small boys. The psychology of pain and obsession which produces this externally absurd contortion of values is as yet withheld from us. The play is not without its rich depths of novelistic psychology, but it eschews the novel's consistency of characterisation in order to pursue its dramatic effects. Shylock's inner pain is not *immediately* exposed to us, and it proves all the more troubling because of that initial withholding.

Indeed, in the planning and execution of her escape, Jessica is more immediately worried, and has more cause to worry, about Lorenzo and herself than about her father. Or is that *for us* to be worrying too much about Lorenzo and Jessica when we should be more simply appreciative and enjoying of their light-hearted vivacity? Are we being tempted into a sombre over-reading of their inner psychology when our attention should rather be on the lively antics of their subplot? One of the great puzzles of *The Merchant of Venice* lies in determining when we should be pondering questions of virtue and when we should be enjoying its theatrical cakes and ale. Certainly, the most *serious* relevance of Lorenzo and Jessica in *The Merchant of Venice* rests not in the characters themselves but in the consequences of their actions for Shylock, consequences which we only begin to see later in the play. But beyond that?

Again it seems appropriate to talk of the defects of Shakespeare's creative virtues. There are perhaps too many couples in the play, all doing too much, for us to determine securely their relative importances and the kind and degree of interpretative scrutiny it is appropriate to bring to bear on them. Moreover, our uncertainty is accentuated by the shifting nature of the play's dramatic idiom, which alternates between, on the one hand, that superb naturalism of dialogue which conveys much more than is actually being said and hints repeatedly at the depths of relationship, and, on the other, the more conventional and stylised language of theatrical comedy. The character about whose mental and emotional state we have just been speculating so intently can suddenly give way to a lightness of rhymes which exposes such speculation as pretentiously humourless. Equally, the stock character's playful conventionalities can suddenly be transformed into words coming from a much more pained individual. Surface liveliness alternates with a depth of human life; the tone even of individual lines can prove extraordinarily difficult to determine; and the range of appropriate responses becomes no less difficult to fix.

In the case of Lorenzo and Jessica, are we to *study* shallow characters or to remain undistracted from larger matters as a result of Shakespeare's deliberately light and superficial characterisation of this couple? It is absurd to ponder over Rosencrantz and Guildenstern as we do over Hamlet, but it is also absurd to berate that pair for not meriting the attention which Hamlet demands. What is and is not absurd in respect of Lorenzo and Jessica is much less clear. Certainly, there is too much individual life in their exchanges for us not to find them distracting, but we must recognise, too, that any resulting theatrical interpretations and critical readings here are extensions rather than realisations of the test. In such cases, our thinking may be initiated and directed by the text's hints, but it may never be fully and substantially corroborated by the textual evidence.

How worried *is* Jessica?

Alack, what heinous sin is it in me
To be asham'd to be my father's child!
But though I am a daughter to his blood,
I am not to his manners. O Lorenzo,
If thou keep promise, I shall end this strife,
Become a Christian and thy loving wife.

(II.iii. 16–21)

'If thou keep promise'—how large an 'if' is that? And, given the neatness of her rhymes, are the doubts which precede them rhetorical or real for Jessica? Certainly, Jessica is in the very odd position of having to put a lot of work and planning into her own abduction. Lorenzo seems to treat the elopement with the same casualness he treats the masque— as something which can be got up in an hour or two. So perhaps he cannot be relied upon to pursue a plan of his own. It is left to Jessica to dot the i's and cross the t's in long, legible letters of campaign:

> She hath directed
> How I shall take her from her father's house;
> What gold and jewels she is furnish'd with;
> What page's suit she hath in readiness . . .
>
> (II.iv. 29–32)

There is a marked contrast in the behaviour of each of the couple in the escape proper. Lorenzo is happy-go-lucky, Jessica more anxiously fussing and garrulous. To what extent may that difference be ascribed merely to girlish nerves, to Jessica's greater inexperience, to the flutter of excitement in anticipation of the long-withheld pleasures of the world, to the residual Jewish officiousness in Shylock's daughter? To what extent does the disparity hint at a more serious imbalance in this match? Certainly, a character who can dismiss her father in the lightness of

> Farewell; and if my fortune be not crost,
> I have a father, you a daughter, lost.
>
> (II.v. 55–6)

is not *worried* by what she is doing, and in turn we, the play's audience, are invited neither to worry nor to tut over her. Lorenzo treats the whole matter with a casualness verging on negligence, but is he *too* casual? Or might a greater show of concern appear inappropriately foppish in the young man about Venice, and inappropriate, too, to the kind of dramatic action of which he is a part? Yet there are suggestions that Jessica's anxiety may be a more serious thing, a vulnerability arising from the recognition that this is the most irrevocably important moment in her life and yet a moment which the Christians—not least Lorenzo—seem barely to have time for. The event is framed by the cynical quips of Solanio, Salerio and Gratiano and by the rush of Bassanio's and Gratiano's departure from Venice. Bent on maintaining Christian innocence in *The Merchant of Venice* C. L. Barber argues that 'Lorenzo's enterprise in stealing

Jessica wins our sympathy partly because it is done in a masque, as a merriment' (Barber 1972, p. 165). But, in the manner characteristic of the play, the masque is promised only to be aborted, and the hurried stage business which sees Lorenzo and Jessica off in their gondola is remote from such leisurely entertainment. Waiting for Lorenzo, his Venetian friends indulge in knowing cynicism about young love's readiness to stale and tire—sentiments not far removed from Cressida's shrewdly street-wise 'Men prize the thing ungain'd more than it is' (*Troilus and Cressida* I.ii. 281). But, when he does finally arrive on the scene, Lorenzo's behaviour does not prove the contrast that we might find in similar circumstances between the lover Romeo and *his* cynically witty friends. There is little of Gratiano's characterisation of the lover as an eager young colt and a lively bark about Lorenzo: Lorenzo is late, and casually so:

> Sweet friends, your patience for my long abode!
> Not I, but my affairs, have made you wait.
> When you shall please to play the thieves for wives,
> I'll watch as long for you then. Approach;
> Here dwells my father Jew. Ho! who's within?
>
> (II.vi. 21–5)

The abrupt nonchalance which characterises Lorenzo's initiation of his future is laughable, but is the Jessica whose double-checking questions reveal her as her father's daughter merely excited or more vulnerably anxious?

> Jessica   Who are you? Tell me, for more certainty,
> Albeit I'll swear that I do know your
>   tongue.
> Lorenzo   Lorenzo, and thy love.
> Jessica   Lorenzo, certain; and my love indeed;
> For who love I so much? And now who
>   knows
> But you, Lorenzo, whether I am yours?

Lorenzo   Heaven and thy thoughts are witness that
                    thou art.

(II.vi. 26–32)

And *Lorenzo's* thoughts? All Jessica's talk here is of the certainty of *her* love. Lorenzo's replies are far from effusive and, while couched in Christian terms of heaven and *eventually* of his 'constant soul', such language may not be the most tactful for this particular protestation and seems chosen in part with an eye to pointing up the religious oddities of the match for his friends' amusement.

There is broad comedy as Shylock's wealth is launched from the window onto the stage. The money involved in so many of the loves in this play is now all too tangibly before us. We may be seeing a straightforwardly adventurous Jessica shrewdly and joyously getting the man *and* getting the money to keep her in the style to which she has not been accustomed. Alternatively, Jessica's concern with money here may be less self-centred, more complex and anxious. She seems more concerned to give it to Lorenzo than she is to take it from Shylock for herself. With some reason, pro-Shylockian critics give Jessica a hard time as the light and unthinkingly prodigal cause of her father's pain. But if Jessica is the cause of suffering—and it is worth remembering that we see that suffering only later in the play—then the text furnishes some evidence of her own vulnerability. She is running off with a man who, if he does feel love for her, feels a love of a shallowness which verges on the inconsequential. Only the priggishly idealistic fail to see that the materially precious can be an eloquent expression of love. But money, gold and jewels can also be a pathetic attempt to buy love and security. And there are things in the play to suggest that Jessica's anxiety is not misplaced:

Here, catch this casket; it is worth the pains.

(II.vi. 33)

It at least is worth the pains. Is Jessica perhaps much less sure of what *she* is worth to Lorenzo? And, when she goes on to gabble nervously about herself, is this merely excited and delightful eye-fluttering or does it betray a need for reassurance which Lorenzo, anxious to have done and get off to the party, neither recognises nor meets?

Jessica	I am glad 'tis night, you do not look on me,
	For I am much asham'd of my exchange;
	But love is blind, and lovers cannot see
	The pretty follies that themselves commit,
	For, if they could, Cupid himself would blush
	To see me thus transformed to a boy.
Lorenzo	Descend, for you must be my torch-bearer.
Jessica	What! must I hold a candle to my shames?
	They in themselves, good sooth, are too too light.
	Why, 'tis an office of discovery, love,
	And I should be obscur'd.
Lorenzo	So are you, sweet,
	Even in the lovely garnish of a boy.
	But come at once,
	For the close night doth play the runaway,
	And we are stay'd for at Bassanio's feast.

(II.vi. 34–48)

Is Jessica merely returning for more loot, or is she redoubling her efforts at a more psychological form of insurance?

> I will make fast the doors, and gild myself
> With some moe ducats, and be with you straight.

(II.vi. 49–50)

I am unsure how far we are to press these lines. The habits of the dutiful daughter are not so easily thrown off, even if,

ironically, Jessica is locking the doors after *she* has bolted
with the loot; but are we to notice too that Jessica does not
bring the ducats with her, but gilds herself with them to
enhance her attractiveness for a Lorenzo whom she is
anxious to placate and incommode no further?

Jessica is rarely mentioned in the play except in terms
which render her identity problematic, ambiguous and
shifting: she is repeatedly defined negatively by denial or
dislocation of the various roles and relationships she
abandons—her race, her religion, her parentage. She is ever
'gentle Jessica', the gentile Jewess, and too easily the material
for the Christians' tediously repetitive jokes about who her
mother and father might be. Subsequent to her departure
with Lorenzo, Jessica is seen by some critics as visually and
significantly present in the silence of forgotten isolation, lost
in the wilderness with her monkey. Ruth Nevo remarks on
the importance of that monkey as the 'sudden mad whim in
Genoa' which is the product of an 'affection-starved,
companionship-starved impulse' (Nevo 1980, p. 118). But
that monkey might equally well be the symptom of a less
individual but no less important human truth, and the point
of the monkey may lie precisely in its arbitrariness and
insignificance. Released from her father's constraints,
Jessica is rushing into the new pleasure of spending money,
and spending money on whatever catches her eye: in the
markets of sixteenth-century Genoa it happens, not
surprisingly, to be the novelty of a monkey. Ralph Berry
sees an important contrast between Shylock and the
daughter 'who voluntarily joins the Christian community
and stands ready to be assimilated. She is not assimilated'.
For the rest of the play Jessica hovers uneasily on the
periphery of Portia's household and 'the central point to
grasp is that Portia *never*, at any time, volunteers a remark to
Jessica alone' (Berry 1985, p. 57). But is this to turn a chorus-
girl into Madame Butterfly? The argument is from absences
and may be too anachronistically democratic in its umbrage
at the imputed failure of social niceties. Belmont society is

decidedly hierarchical, and Jessica is remote from Portia in
both social and dramatic importance. Moreover, in many of
the play's later scenes, urgent events are afoot which not
merely excuse but require the foregoing of such leisured
civilities.

Readers may find this interpretative toing and froing over
Jessica merely irritating, but its uncertainty represents an
attempt to reflect the uncertainty of the text itself. We are
continually half-hearing deeper resonances in Jessica, both
because locally her language repeatedly suggests a
groundedness and specificity beyond the conventional, and
because other parts of the play have educated our ears to
anticipate the cadences of individual psychology. Listening
to Lorenzo's and Jessica's exchanges in the second half of the
play resembles nothing as much as listening to the trivial
banter of a married couple at a dinner party; we can never
quite relax into a full enjoyment of the wit for fear that it
might just have an edge to it.

One moment in the play focuses our interpretative
difficulty over Jessica. In Act 3 Scene 2 Lorenzo's and
Jessica's arrival in Belmont coincides with the arrival of the
news of Antonio's misfortunes and consequent peril back
in Venice. Jessica, listening to this account of her father's
villainy, makes but one contribution to the anxious
discussions of Shylock's intentions:

> When I was with him, I have heard him swear
> To Tubal and to Chus, his countrymen,
> That he would rather have Antonio's flesh
> Than twenty times the value of the sum
> That he did owe him; and I know, my Lord,
> If law, authority, and power, deny not,
> It will go hard with poor Antonio.
>
> (III.ii. 286–92)

Graham Bradshaw has pointed out that 'In the period
between the signing of the bond and her own elopement,

Jessica had neither the time nor the opportunity to overhear any conversation between her father and his cronies. If we have attended to that time-scale which Shakespeare took such pains to establish, Jessica must be lying' (Bradshaw 1986, p. 100). Bradshaw concludes that an interpretation which assumes that we positively register this temporal discrepancy is over-ingenious, but he finds the slip on Shakespeare's part interesting and, in many ways, continuous with the play's intentions. He is concerned primarily with the ways in which Jessica's declaration might have an influence upon our view of Shylock and the Christians, and these issues we shall consider later. Here we are concerned with Jessica.

It is plausible to suggest that we do not pay much attention to who is speaking here: the emphatic speech reflects, not on character, but on the urgency of the situation. If we *do* wonder why it is *Jessica* who characterises Shylock's malevolence in such detail, then, whether or not we register that it is literally a lie, there is a falsity in Jessica's speaking here. It is over-vehement, over-long and too specific—'To Tubal and to Chus, his countrymen'—and it is too eager to advertise its own loyalties—'*his* countrymen . . . *my* lord . . . *poor* Antonio'. Jessica's overwillingness to please only reinforces her undignified isolation. Betrayal, once embarked upon, can only be compounded in the kind of cruelty of which the vulnerable are especially capable.

Potentially at least, in *The Merchant of Venice* there is an antithesis between father and daughter. If Shylock suffers because of a self-isolating assertion of self, then Jessica's willingness to assimilate herself into the Christian world denies her integrity and reduces her to a frivolity. Neither extremity is happy, but perhaps as the play reveals to us more and more of this Venetian world, we may begin to doubt whether any compromise is available to the Jews who are in it but not of it.

·5·
Caskets

Much of the play's power stems from its sustaining of two centres of action in Venice and in Belmont, and in its continual cutting between these two worlds lies much of its suspense and tension—and some of its oddities and uncertainties. Subsequent to Act 2, *The Merchant of Venice* proves no less complicated, but it now manages a more sustained focus—first, on the scene where Bassanio makes his choice of caskets before Venetian anxieties quickly arrive to encroach on the Belmont world and, secondly, on the Venetian trial scene where Belmont, in the shape of Portia, comes to the rescue of the Venetians.

In Act 3 each world proves equally anxious, though in contrasting ways, about matters of love and money: Bassanio must make a successful choice of casket; Shylock is left to react to the interrelated losses of his daughter and his ducats. The two worlds, pivoting on the unhappy lot of the unhappy Antonio, bound to both Bassanio and Shylock, are set on a course which promises violent collision. The central scene of declared love between Portia and Bassanio is a curious scene, initially very powerful, but soon interrupted and promising much more than is finally realised in the play. Marked by a lyricism which gestures beyond language, 'carried beyond expression, using words to tell of being beyond them' (Barber 1972, p. 176), it is yet enclosed by two appearances of the insistently literalistic Shylock. More than that, it is itself disrupted by the harsh news of the crisis in Venice which presses in on Belmont's celebrations. This juxtaposition of two contrasting dramatic idioms, and of the characters' opposing ways with words, points the main dilemma for interpreters of *The Merchant of Venice*: how far are we to attend with a precise Shylockian ear to the words and terms of the play, and how far are we to allow its music, mood and magic to override such literalism? Again, the opposition is between the letter and the spirit, between rigour and accommodating flexibility.

This Act begins in Venice with a further example of the play's intimations of potential violence in the news of Antonio's ship 'wreck'd on the narrow seas', and it is dramatically appropriate that the 'old carrion', Shylock, should encroach threateningly on such news. But, stumbling on this Venetian gossip, Shylock is quite preoccupied by losses of his own, and it is the tauntings of Solanio and Salerio which turn Shylock's mind to Antonio: the Venetians half-create the monster who is to oppress them. In the play's first scene, Solanio and Salerio's leisured boredom had relieved itself comically in their interrogation of Antonio. Now, not deliberately but unthinkingly, their curiosity and malicious amusement channel Shylock's mind towards revenge. Significantly, Shylock treats their initial inquiry regarding his knowledge of Antonio's misfortune as a dispiriting distraction—'There I have another bad match'—before he latches relentlessly onto 'let him look to his bond', as if by tenaciously chewing on the lesser pain, Shylock may relieve the greater. But, while right in respect of what this reveals of Shylock's particular and immediate intention, H. B. Charlton is surely too ready to protest the unequivocal innocence of Shylock's general disposition:

> The badness of the bargain is all Shylock is aware of: and the bargain is only bad if Shylock had meant it merely in the way of ordinary business. If for a second he had

thought of it as a means to gratify his hatred—the only
way in which in the legend he ever did think of it—he
could never have described it as a 'bad bargain', but
clearly as an unbelievably fortunate one.

(Charlton 1949, p. 150)

However, if not innocent and not solely the product of
this particular abuse, A. D. Moody's larger perspective
reminds us that Shylock's malevolence remains 'a direct
consequence of the way the Christians abuse him' (Moody
1964, p. 30). In a moment, Shylock's résumé of Antonio's
past behaviour will explicitly recall as much. And the abuse
goes on. When Shylock rises to Solanio's and Salerio's
initial taunts in this scene, the tactless Venetians cannot
contain themselves: 'Why, I am sure, if he forfeit, thou wilt
not take his flesh. What's that good for?' (III.i. 43–4). In the
famous speech which follows, justifying a course of revenge
which even now is only hypothetical, the Shylock who
previously had doggedly asserted his difference in a
confusion of resentment and pride, now insists no less
doggedly on his common humanity:

And what's his reason? I am a Jew. Hath not a Jew eyes?
Hath not a Jew hands, organs, dimensions, senses,
affections, passions, fed with the same food, hurt with the
same weapons, subject to the same diseases, healed by the
same means, warmed and cooled by the same winter and
summer, as a Christian is? If you prick us, do we not
bleed? If you tickle us, do we not laugh? If you poison us,
do we not die? And if you wrong us, shall we not revenge?
If we are like you in the rest, we will resemble you in that.
If a Jew wrong a Christian, what is his humility? Revenge.
If a Christian wrong a Jew, what should his sufferance be
by Christian example? Why, revenge. The villainy you
teach me I will execute; and it shall go hard but I will
better the instruction.

(III.i. 50–62)

Shylock's sense of his own identity is unrelentingly physical, and his sense of relationship reductive. The truth and adequacy of words rests not solely in themselves but in the situation from which they emanate, in the character who speaks them and in the characters to whom they are addressed. The perverse but powerful relevance of this speech arises from the disjunctions rather than the appropriate combinings of these criteria. It is true that this speech 'wrings sympathy even from those who elsewhere grudge [Shylock] a particle of it' (Goddard 1960, p. 98). But if this were all it were innocently intended to achieve, then here Shylock would be uncharacteristically foregoing his dignity to the point where he becomes whimperingly pathetic in the lesser sense of that word. It is true, too, that 'it is a pathos which, as the speech moves, converts to menace' (Barber 1972, pp. 181–2). But the fact of its menace does not insulate us from its truth; indeed, a large part of its menace comes directly from our recognition of the truth of its diagnosis of the play's Christians. Shylock's tenaciously repetitive rhetoric worries itself towards the one perverse question: 'And if you wrong us, shall we not revenge?' If we recall Shylock's 'This is kind I offer', the semantic slide from reciprocation to retaliation is fully explicit here. If we are worried by the implications of Portia's 'It is a good divine that follows his own instructions' for the Christians, and come to suspect, in the course of the play, some laxity and want of integrity in these Christians, then the rigour of Shylock's 'The villainy you teach me I will execute; and it shall go hard but I will better the instruction' is no less unhappy. Shylock is bound by his literalism to the point where it proves dehumanising for himself and threatens to destroy others, notably Antonio. Shylock's subsequent brief appearance when he encounters Antonio and the Gaoler, reveals him not merely deaf to dialogue but shouting others down, his own voice contracted to automaton-like reiteration.

I'll have my bond; speak not against my bond.
I have sworn an oath that I will have my bond.
. . .
I'll have my bond. I will not hear thee speak;
I'll have my bond; and therefore speak no more.
. . .
I'll have no speaking; I will have my bond.

(III.iii. 4–17)

Shylock is so bound by his own words as to render communication impossible. The justification of his revenge which Salerio and Solanio provoke in the first scene of Act 3 is both unanswerable in its logic and intolerable in its exclusion of human sympathy. And these two Venetians, if their shallowness allows them a full realisation of what their earlier casual taunts have nurtured, can only be grateful for the arrival of Antonio's message which removes them from Shylock's presence.

The play itself creaks here with the cheapness of its cue for Tubal's entrance—a cue characteristic of the Christians but lame none the less: 'Here comes another of the tribe; a third cannot be match'd, unless the devil himself turn Jew' (III. i. 66–7). In the Venetian scenes in particular, *The Merchant of Venice* overplays the advantage of the setting in the city's streets which licenses chance encounters, and, at times, an excess of plot, information and minor characters obstructs the full realisation of the play's inner life. Tubal's arrival in the play is such a case. In showing how Tubal goads Shylock further, Shakespeare seems to be fudging the issue. The creation of Tubal seems a sign of the dramatist's reluctance to allow a complete substantiation of the intimated link between the Christians' mistreatment of Shylock and the Jew's plot for revenge. Such reluctance may be the understandable result of Shakespeare's fear of upsetting the tonal balance of the play and blackening his Christian protagonists to the extent that the audience is alienated from the comic pleasures of their romantic fates.

Having uncovered in Shylock the greater reality underlying the stereotypical Jew, and having gone half way to an analysis which locates the play's darknesses and evil, not in a single villain but, more interestingly, in the larger interactions of Venetian society and its various groups, Shakespeare subjects that larger exploration to a temporary arrest and introduces a thinner, more manageable agent of the play's evil in the form of another Jewish stereotype, Tubal. We continue to see the developing psychology of Shylock's revenge, but by way of an altogether more external mechanism.

Tubal is one of the most uninterestingly unpleasant minor roles in Shakespeare. Here the play's own insights can be turned against it: hath not a Tubal eyes? Apparently not, for Tubal, measured against the play's other minor roles, the Nerissas, Moroccos and Gratianos, merits no more than half a scene and a couple of dishonourable mentions. He remains a device. At odds with the play's more inward and individual characterisation, Tubal functions as the etiolated remnant of a Vice from a Morality play: he delivers his pluses and minuses, his good news of Antonio's misfortune and his bad news of Jessica's profligacy, in the inert prose of painfully obvious manipulation. Shylock *is* preoccupied. Tubal *is*, supposedly, his Jewish friend (and it is indicative of the vulgarity of the play's lapse here that it should need friends like this to deflect our scrutiny of Shylock's Christian enemies). But, given these concessions, it remains telling that Shylock, himself a great manipulator and ever alert to the manoeuvrings of others, should remain unaware of what Tubal is up to here. The only explanation can be that Tubal is not to be thought of in this way and is functioning, not as a character, but merely as a mouth with no mind behind it. Tubal's machinations culminate in the reminder:

> *Tubal*   But Antonio is certainly undone.
> *Shylock*   Nay, that's true; that's very true. Go, Tubal,

fee me an officer; bespeak him a fortnight
before. I will have the heart of him, if he
forfeit . . .

(III.i. 107–11).

Here, if we need to pin it down, is the precise moment when
Shylock's schemes for revenge harden into resolve. In a play
elsewhere so subtle, such a moment can only come as a
disappointment. The play's interrogative method meets in
Tubal the blank wall of literary mechanism, and, by
extension, the intelligent Shylock is here in danger of being
reduced to a Pavlovian dog. One particularly unpleasant
and unintended irony, ministering to gentile complacency,
which results here is that Shylock is tortured, not by the
Christians, but by his fellow Jews, Jessica and Tubal. The
Jew is revealed to have a heart only for other Jews to crush it.
In this scene the play does not so much expose prejudice as
transfer it.

Even in such uninteresting company, Shylock himself
remains interesting. It is common to assume that Shylock's
error is to confuse money and love. But the play never
allows *any* of its characters that sharp division between
love's wealth and material wealth which John Russell Brown
describes (Brown 1962, pp. 45–81). It might initially appear
that Shylock's exclamations here reveal a desire to recoup
his ducats at the expense, the extreme expense, of his
daughter: 'I would my daughter were dead at my foot, and
the jewels in her ear; would she were hears'd at my foot, and
the ducats in her coffin!' (III.i. 77–80). But Shylock here is
destructive rather than possessive. The contortion of
destructive feeling is self-laceratingly directed at *both*
daughter and ducats. The pain of the double loss and the
tormenting uncertainties which the loss occasions are such
that Shylock seeks perverse relief in the fanciful desire that
both daughter and ducats are irrevocably and utterly
destroyed: *both* are to be hearsed and trampled under foot as
the pain of their absence distorts itself into the escapist wish

that *both* had never existed. Harold C. Goddard makes the point in his characteristically one-sided sentimental way:

> That tormented cry is usually taken as meaning, 'I would give my daughter's life to get my ducats back'. And doubtless that is what Shylock thinks he is saying. But note that it is not Jessica dead and the ducats locked up in his vault. The ducats are in the coffin too! Plainly an unconscious wish to bury his own miserliness. Shylock is ripe for a better life.
>
> (Goddard 1960, p. 96)

The current of Shylock's feeling here, while profoundly human, is remorselessly negative. There is no sub-Freudian slip ripening into a better future for a life in which emotional riches, no less than material ones, are now lost in the past:

> Tubal   One of them showed me a ring that he had
>   of your daughter for a monkey.
> Shylock   Out upon her! Thou torturest me, Tubal. It
>   was my turquoise; I had it of Leah when I
>   was a bachelor; I would not have given it for
>   a wilderness of monkeys.
>
> (III.i. 101–6)

Through the provocation, first of the Christians, and subsequently of Tubal, two subjects—Shylock's own losses and Antonio's losses—are brought to coalesce in Shylock's unsettled brain. The emotional intensity and the confusions which produce Shylock's inhumanity are a black parody of the feelings of the equally transported and giddily confused Portia and Bassanio whom we are about to see. The juxtaposition of Shylock and the lovers in Act 3 shows two kinds of 'madness' and unsettled senses. Both kinds of reaction are in response to matters of love, and while these extreme responses are opposed and antagonistic, we are compelled to recognise that both are the product of *human* feeling and *human* need. Shylock is frightening because he is akin: his evil is recognisably and understandably human. Ironically, the resources of vilification and prejudice which the Christians deploy to shield themselves from that recognition of Shylock's humanity will serve, finally, to confirm that kinship in its uglier form. These antagonists are bound together in their unkindness.

While Shylock narrows into obsession, Portia and Bassanio grow into a generosity of reciprocated feeling, and this is reflected in the opulent formality of their setting, its music, the register of their language and the characteristic movement of the verse they speak. But Portia's and Bassanio's love is not without urgencies of its own. The constraints habitually present in the first anxious moments of mutual declaration are accentuated by the particular circumstances of the story in which Portia and Bassanio find themselves. Declarations of love involve vulnerability and self-risk for the declarer. Such occasions, moreover, often involve a paradoxical mingling of the desires to prolong the moment and to seize the time. The feelings of the lovers at this point in *The Merchant of Venice* are intensified by the external and extreme conditions of Portia's father's will and the casket test. That test is a considerable risk and reminds us that the couple, and Bassanio in particular, have a great deal to lose. The subjective and anxious intensities of feeling which are so often the concern of the love-poet are here objectified by the terms of the dramatist's story, and the casket plot, however improbable it may appear in summary, is now entirely congruent with the reality of inner feeling. Portia says:

> I pray you tarry; pause a day or two
> Before you hazard; for, in choosing wrong,
> I lose your company; therefore forbear awhile.
> There's something tells me—but it is not love—
> I would not lose you; and you know yourself
> Hate counsels not in such a quality.

But lest you should not understand me well—
And yet a maiden hath no tongue but thought—
I would detain you here some month or two
Before you venture for me. I could teach you
How to choose right, but then I am forsworn;
So will I never be; so may you miss me;
But if you do, you'll make me wish a sin,
That I had been forsworn. Beshrew your eyes!
They have o'erlooked me and divided me;
One half of me is yours, the other half yours—
Mine own, I would say; but if mine, then yours,
And so all yours. O! these naughty times
Puts bars between the owners and their rights;
And so, though yours, not yours. Prove it so,
Let fortune go to hell for it, not I.
I speak too long, but 'tis to peize the time,
To eke it, and to draw it out in length,
To stay you from election.

                                         (III.ii. 1–24)

Portia's first expression of anxious procrastination, of
urgency of feeling constrained by modesty and fear, is
precisely mirrored in the phrasing and movement of the
verse here. The underlying impulse towards the free flow of
emotion is registered in the tendency towards
enjambement, but it is checked by the frequent and heavy
pauses coming in the middle of the lines, and by the
abruptness with which Portia repeatedly breaks off into
parenthetical qualification and tangential exclamation. The
connectives are habitually the 'buts' and 'yets' of constraint,
and the speech prolongs itself in synonymous repetition.
Portia's self-consciousness is reflected in the consciousness
of her own language (particularly her pronouns), which
interrupts and entangles the free expression of her feelings.
Nervous loquacity is at odds with reticent obscurity.

But the fineness of the poetry in this scene is intermittent.
Bassanio, prior to his winning of Portia, has much less to say

than his love, and seems more content to rest, unselfconsciously, in conventionalities of expression. He is 'upon the rack', protests that treason and his love are opposed like 'snow and fire', and rather weakly transforms Portia's 'confess and live' into ' "Confess" and "love" '. He also seems better able to talk to himself than to address Portia, as if he were not at home in the dramatic idiom which she establishes in this scene. Whether these lapses are to be attributed to the fitful nature of Shakespeare's inspiration here, or whether they are a deliberate illumination of character and an indication of an imbalance in the relationship, is difficult to determine. But Bassanio is initially unforthcoming, and perhaps his eagerness to get on with the choice is in excess of what a full recognition of the solemnity and importance of that choice might allow.

At any rate, it is Portia who has to draw Bassanio into the reciprocity of word play, and such witty dalliance has, for Portia at least, a serious purpose of prolongation and delay. Moreover, in its talk of racks, treason, torture and mistrust, such language is not without a latent violence, and these metaphors' effectiveness derives, in part, from our knowledge of the threat to Antonio attendant on this love-venture. As is typical of the comedies generally, Shakespeare is rediscovering the expressive life in the images and tropes of conventional love poetry, and such language has again gripped a particular reality.

In those suspenseful moments, as Bassanio prepares to make his choice among the caskets, Portia requests music which enhances the idealistic and romantic qualities of the moment. Her succeeding disquisition on the nature of music emphasises its role as high ceremonial art, appropriate to the most serious events in human life:

Let music sound while he doth make his choice;
Then, if he lose, he makes a swan-like end,
Fading in music. That the comparison
May stand more proper, my eye shall be the stream

And wat'ry death-bed for him. He may win;
And what is music then? Then music is
Even as the flourish when true subjects bow
To a new-crowned monarch; such it is
As are those dulcet sounds in break of day
That creep into the dreaming bridegroom's ear
And summon him to marriage.

                                        (III.ii. 43–53)

Music turns to song:

>   Tell me where is fancy bred,
>   Or in the heart or in the head,
>   How begot, how nourished?
>   Reply, reply.
>   It is engend'red in the eyes,
>   With gazing fed; and fancy dies
>   In the cradle where it lies.
>   Let us all ring fancy's knell:
>   I'll begin it—Ding, dong, bell.
> *All*   Ding, dong, bell.

                                        (III.ii. 63–72)

The theme of this song bears directly on the nature of
romantic love, both as it is explored in this play and in
Shakespeare's romantic comedies generally. Thus, for
example, we recognise echoes of *A Midsummer Night's
Dream*'s sustained exploration of the nature of the
imagination and the subjectivity involved in the acts of
loving and valuing. The song's theme has a more particular
relevance for the scene in which it occurs: it illuminates
Bassanio's choice, and the test which involves
discrimination between appearance and substance.
Formally too, the song's structure of question and reply
parallels the form of Bassanio's test.

In pondering his choice, Bassanio sombrely takes up the
song's interest in appearance and valuing, in a solemnly
philosophical meditation, prompted in this singularly

ungrave character, by the gravity of the occasion. His rhetorical questions touch resonantly and multiply on moments, actions and characters throughout the play: on the gracious but tainted voice of law (Portia?); on the religious error approved by the fair text (Shylock and Antonio on usury?); on the bearded and frowning Herculean cowards (Morocco?); on beauty 'purchas'd by the weight' (Lorenzo and Jessica?); and on the 'guiled shore' by the 'most dangerous sea' (the precariousness of mercantile ventures?). These allusions play over the whole drama, but here they are insufficiently directed for their relevance to take on any telling specificity; the literalistic and logical precision required in their working out seems excessive and inappropriate in this context. The ironic points potentially present are somehow deprived of their sharpness by the urgency of the situation in which they occur and our more immediate concern about the choice which is about to be made. The latent and dark underside of the play is curiously held in check here by its immediate and romantic surface. At the point where we are told by Bassanio that 'The world is still deceiv'd with ornament', we are indeed attending more to the ornament of the test's formal setting and the gracious voices and fair outward parts of the test's participants—though 'surface' and 'ornament' do not do full justice to the inner reality of Portia's and perhaps Bassanio's feelings. Alexander Leggatt's account of what is happening here seems immediately right, even if, away from the potency of the scene we might be worried to press such terms as 'instinctive wisdom', 'paradox' and 'inner logic' when they are set in opposition to 'logical thought':

> rational thought is set against instinctive wisdom, and the latter is seen as the surer guide. The paradox of Bassanio's success is that he is at once a more down-to-earth character than the other suitors and one whose mind is more finely attuned to the workings of convention. In the

speech in which he meditates on his choice, he says
nothing about himself as an individual, or Portia as an
individual; he ignores all the inscriptions, and thereby
avoids the dead-end traps of logical thought. Instead, his
mind moves instinctively to the inner logic of the
convention . . .

(Leggatt 1974, p. 133)

The choice successfully made, anxiety gives way to a
controlled and eloquent outpouring of an abundance of
feeling:

> *Portia* [*Aside*]   How all the other passions fleet to air,
>   As doubtful thoughts, and rash embrac'd
>   despair,
>   And shudd'ring fear, and green-eyed
>   jealousy!
>   O love, be moderate, allay thy ecstasy,
>   In measure rain thy joy, scant this excess!
>   I feel too much thy blessing. Make it less,
>   For fear I surfeit.
>
> (III.ii. 108–14)

Hesitation is now supplanted by exclamation and excited
question, giving repeated expression to the giddiness of
radically new experience:

> *Bassanio* [*opening the leaden casket*]   What find I here?
>   Fair Portia's counterfeit! What demi-god
>   Hath come so near creation? Move these
>   eyes?
>   Or whether riding on the balls of mine
>   Seem they in motion?
>
> (III.ii. 114–18)

Momentarily at least, Bassanio's sense of the particularity of
his feelings has caught up with Portia's, and he is no longer

prepared to allow the conventionalities of language to serve
as an adequate expression of them:

> Madam, you have bereft me of all words;
> Only my blood speaks to you in my veins . . .
>
> (III.ii. 176–7)

He is 'Giddy in spirit, still gazing in a doubt', experiencing
'such confusion in [his] powers' where 'every something,
being blent together,/Turns to a wild of nothing, save of
joy/Express'd and not express'd'.

The immediate rightness of Portia's account of herself
before Bassanio, derives from a mixture of exaggeration and
modesty which eschews a literal account of the facts of the
matter but exploits the luxury of fiction to give expression
to an extremity of feeling:

> You see me, Lord Bassanio, where I stand,
> Such as I am. Though for myself alone
> I would not be ambitious in my wish
> To wish myself much better, yet for you
> I would be trebled twenty times myself,
> A thousand times more fair, ten thousand times more
>   rich,
> That only to stand high in your account
> I might in virtues, beauties, livings, friends,
> Exceed account. But the full sum of me
> Is sum of something which, to term in gross,
> Is an unlesson'd girl, unschool'd, unpractis'd;
> Happy in this, she is not yet so old
> But she may learn; happier than this,
> She is not bred so dull but she can learn;
> Happiest of all is that her gentle spirit
> Commits itself to yours to be directed,
> As from her lord, her governor, her king.
> Myself and what is mine to you and yours
> Is now converted.
>
> (III.ii. 149–68)

We can measure the distance between Portia's declaration and Shylock's way of seeing the world by saying that, depending on one's point of view, these words either transcend or ignore the kind of reality that meets a Shylockian eye. Portia is neither materially nor spiritually poor in the way she implies; nor is she 'unlesson'd . . . unschool'd, unpractis'd'. The gap between Portia and Shylock registers itself in their attitude to, and use of, words in giving expression to themselves—one character flowingly extravagant, the other insistently and narrowly literalistic. We can measure the distance, too, between Portia and the shadowly sketched Jessica, whom we have seen in the play and who, less sure of Lorenzo's love, must emphatically 'gild' herself with stolen ducats. Portia can divest herself of such accoutrements to stand unadorned, the 'sum of something', paradoxically because she has confidence, first, in Bassanio's reciprocated love and, secondly, in her own spiritual and material wealth. Put crudely, and in a spirit remote from her own words, Portia has enough money to make money irrelevant. Her complete self-possession allows her to give herself so fully to another. Here, in one of the play's many instances of self-definition, Portia has the security to describe herself—'Such as I am'—openly, vulnerably, accommodatingly with neither loss of dignity nor manipulative intention. But, if we are to measure the Shylocks, Antonios and Jessicas against her, we must recall that these characters have no such security, and that their sense of themselves is a less easy thing and enjoys no such straightforwardly harmonious relation to the society in which they struggle to exist.

The moment of Portia's and Bassanio's harmony is infectious; it spreads beyond the couple themselves, but, in doing so, it is diluted into the more comic ordinariness of Gratiano's and Nerissa's betrothal. The latter has been a wooing conducted, we infer, in less eloquent and more taxing terms:

You saw the mistress, I beheld the maid;
You lov'd, I lov'd . . .
. . .
. . . wooing here until I sweat again,
And swearing till my very roof was dry
With oaths of love, at last—if promise last—
I got a promise of this fair one here
To have her love, provided that your fortune
Achiev'd her mistress.

(III.ii. 199–209)

Bassanio finds his tongue again, and the tone and mood of
the scene modulate further through the bawdy humour of
the two couples' wager over the first boy into the arrival of
Bassanio's Venetian friends when, in Bassanio's
embarrassment, we sense that Portia's gift of 'This house,
these servants, and this same myself' is being taken and
made free with too immediately and too literally:

Bassanio   Lorenzo and Salerio, welcome hither,
           If that the youth of my new int'rest here
           Have power to bid you welcome. By your
                 leave,
           I bid my very friends and countrymen,
           Sweet Portia, welcome.

(III.ii. 222–6)

We are not allowed to linger long over Portia and Bassanio
in their rare and rarest moments. More people than Shylock
are pressing rudely in on the couple's new world, even in its
earliest moments, but it is the Shylockian threat which
gradually forces the dominant idiom of these characters
back to the literal and the basic. Blood and violence are
indicated metaphorically here:

Portia   There are some shrewd contents in yond
                 same paper

> That steals the colour from Bassanio's
> cheek.
>
> . . .
>
> *Bassanio*   . . . Here is a letter, lady,
> The paper as the body of my friend,
> And every word in it a gaping wound
> Issuing life-blood.
>
> (III.ii. 245–68)

But the metaphors gradually come back to the precise fact of
the threat to Antonio's flesh. With the coming of such news,
Bassanio is forced to give an account of himself less attentive
to the quality of feeling in his love and answering more
practically and precisely to the circumstances of his wooing.
The full story, told too soon, mingles love with more
mundane regards:

> Gentle lady,
> When I did first impart my love to you,
> I freely told you all the wealth I had
> Ran in my veins—I was a gentleman;
> And then I told you true. And yet, dear lady,
> Rating myself at nothing, you shall see
> How much I was a braggart. When I told you
> My state was nothing, I should then have told you
> That I was worse than nothing; for indeed
> I have engag'd myself to a dear friend,
> Engag'd my friend to his mere enemy,
> To feed my means.
>
> (III.ii. 254–65)

There is something disillusioning and deceiving in the
discovery that Bassanio was not free to be the person he
offered himself as. And Portia's self-possession and
linguistic extravagance are now translated into unthinking
confidence and a more mundane monetary extravagance as
she, believing that the problem will be resolved by throwing
money at it, underestimates the nature of Shylock's threat:

Portia	What sum owes he the Jew?
Bassanio	For me, three thousand ducats.
Portia	What! no more?

Pay him six thousand, and deface the bond;
Double six thousand, and then treble that,
. . .
. . . You shall have gold
To pay the petty debt twenty times over.

(III.ii. 299–308)

Portia's and Bassanio's love no longer transcends the more ordinary world; it now appears too remotely and too complacently above it.

Indeed, other critics have responded quite differently to the *entirety* of this love scene, and are never to be seduced by its music. Viewing Portia's and Bassanio's declarations of love in the larger context of the whole play, such critics' eyes are on the discrepant rather than the harmonious. They record not what is immediately before them but what they see as significantly and ironically absent. Harold C. Goddard is not to be fooled by the scene's extravagances. He finds that

> when Bassanio stands in front of the golden casket, clad in the rich raiment that Antonio's (i.e., Shylock's) gold has presumably bought, and addresses it,
>
> > Therefore, thou gaudy gold,
> > Hard food for Midas, I will none of thee,
>
> we feel that if Shakespeare did not intend the irony it got in in spite of him. No, gold, I'll have none of thee, Bassanio declares (whether he knows it or not), except a bit from Antonio-Shylock to start me going, and a bit from a certain lady 'richly left' whose dowry shall repay the debts of my youth and provide for my future. Beyond that, none.

Who chooseth me must give and hazard all he hath.

It is almost cruel to recall the inscription on the casket
Bassanio picked in the light of what he *received* from
Shylock and of what he let Antonio *risk* in his behalf.
                                        (Goddard 1960, p. 86)

Are we being irresponsible in allowing, in this scene, out of
sight to be out of mind? Or is it carpingly pedantic to be
always asking where the money comes from?
    A. D. Moody is similarly sharp-eyed:

Bassanio appears in the most gorgeous fashion of a
courtly suitor . . . putting on a goodly outside as he has
advised Gratiano to do, and as Portia will do for the trial.
. . . His appearance is belied in almost all that he says, so
that he shows up very badly in comparison with
Morocco's gentle courtliness. . . . [H]is moralisings upon
ornament are most clearly relevant to himself, his state
nothing, but gilded with borrowed wealth.
                                        (Moody 1964, p. 35)

Moody finds in Bassanio a grotesque mixture of self-
righteousness and cynicism. But, if Moody and Goddard
are right, in what ways are we enjoying this play and what
kind of pleasure is it giving us?
    Such embarrassments arise from the animus some critics
direct against Bassanio. But Portia, too, is not exempt from
their attentions. It is this scene which provides the oddest
interpretative crux of the play. For some critics the song
which Portia requests as a prelude to Bassanio's choice of
caskets has a much more mundane relevance than those I
have enumerated above, and we are hearing, not elegant
cadences, but the aural equivalent of a dig in the ribs: '. . .
bred . . . head . . . nourished' rhyme with 'lead', and Portia is
giving a hint to ring a different kind of bell in Bassanio's head
from those in the song's refrain.

The way critics divide over this is predictably in keeping with the larger emphases of their interpretations. Thus C. L. Barber is Portia-like in the grandeur of his dismissal: 'The notion that [the song] serves as a signal to warn Bassanio off gold and silver is one of those busy-body emendations which eliminate the dramatic in seeking to elaborate it' (Barber 1972, p. 174). Harold C. Goddard is so certain that the song 'of course gives away the secret' that he is prepared to be forgiving: 'In view of her father's scheme for selecting her husband, no one will blame Portia for giving Bassanio several hints on the choice of the right casket'. He finds additional evidence in Portia's 'hazard' (III.ii. 2), echoing the lead casket's inscription (Goddard 1960, p. 102). But this is at the very beginning of the scene, and if it does plausible damage to Portia's and Bassanio's moral probity, then it does incredible wonders for Bassanio's intellectual and aural acuity. A. D. Moody is convinced that 'it becomes quite unbelievable that [Bassanio] should have chosen [the lead casket] unprompted . . . that the song gives him the hint is plain enough. . . . To leave no doubt of it the sound of the tolling bell and the references to Fancy dying both evoke the lead in which the dead were folded' (Moody 1964, p. 36).

If we attend to the *situation*, to its third place in the series of three tests, and to its idiom, then it is difficult for us to worry that Bassanio could possibly get his choice of casket wrong, or to feel that he has need of any such hint. If we attend to *character*, and to the more facile aspects of Bassanio's character, it is all too easy to see how Portia might worry that Bassanio needs all the help he can get. Portia has shown her skill as a covert messenger twice before. Bassanio recorded his earlier encounter with her when:

> Sometimes from her eyes
> I did receive fair speechless messages.
>
> (I.i. 163–4)

And, for fear of acquiring the bibulous young German

suitor, Portia had earlier suggested that Nerissa might muddy rather than clarify the casket code:

> Therefore, for fear of the worst, I pray thee set a deep glass of Rhenish wine on the contrary casket; for if the devil be within and that temptation without, I know he will choose it. I will do anything, Nerissa, ere I will be married to a sponge.
>
> (I.ii. 83–8)

But if we are to protest the innocence of Portia's expressed attraction and wit respectively in these cases—as I would be inclined to do—we might recall, too, that Shylock's early and general wish regarding Antonio—'If I can catch him once upon the hip'—might be accorded a similar vindication.

Portia's supposed hint in the song has a precedent in the play's sources: in *Il Pecorone*, the lady's maid gives the hint to Giannetto, Bassanio's literary predecessor, who thereby manages to avoid the drugged wine and stay awake to 'enjoy' his lady as a precondition of winning her. Such a detail belongs, not to the high romance of the casket test, but to the carnal realism of the fabliau world. I have suggested that some of *The Merchant of Venice*'s incongruities arise from Shakespeare's combining of source materials radically different in kind. Here we have a focal point of such difficulties, the difficulty of determining to which kind of world and which kind of story Portia and Bassanio more credibly belong. And such difficulties are of course accentuated by the typical Shakespearean intimations of a psychological depth to such characterisation.

The Arden editor marshals a number of arguments against the intended presence of any hint in the song (Brown 1961, p. 80). Some of his points are weakened by his predisposition to think well of Portia and Bassanio: he takes Portia at her word, reminding us that she 'has said she will not direct Bassanio'. But, others might say, such contradiction between word and deed is only in character. 'It would belittle Bassanio and Portia and cheapen the themes of the play'. But that might be precisely the ironic point. Bassanio's speech of thirty-four lines which follows the song 'would be an odd elaboration if he believed the song had given him the secret'. But others might argue that Bassanio is entirely capable of such dissimulation. More uncontroversially persuasive is Brown's argument that 'In other plays where a character *sings* a secret that he is forbidden to *speak*, the hint is very much broader than here'. Thus, even if intended, that intention is insufficiently present in the text.

This apparently niggling and local difficulty is worth labouring because of its representativeness in respect of the puzzling nature of *The Merchant of Venice* as a whole. Neither reading of this local point seems in keeping with the totality of the play; curiously, it is an awareness of *both* possible readings here which answers most fully to our sense of that puzzling overall complexity. Yet no production and no interpretation can sustain both possibilities within a larger coherence. In practice, it seems impossible for any performance of the play to convey the presence of the song's hint without doing violence to the general tenor and texture of the scene in which it occurs. To attend to the hinting words, we must be tone deaf both to the music which accompanies them, and to the larger music of the scene's lyricism.

And this leads to the largest point which I would risk regarding *The Merchant of Venice*: the play's distinctive power resides in its complexity and ambiguity, but such complexity, while it is cultivated by the inquiring dramatist, is not fully under Shakespeare's control. *The Merchant of Venice* is finally a play of extraordinarily fine moments, rather than the larger coherence of a well-made play—a collage rather than a painting. This is not to say that it is merely a collection of anthology pieces or an invitation to an unrelated series of dramatic *tours de force*. Individual scenes

derive much of their power from their place within a larger
unit but are finally not to be summed up into a larger unity.
The play's transitions are sometimes happily productive of
telling juxtapositions, and sometimes merely awkward.
And a full response to all of its particular finenesses requires
a degree of forgetfulness which the aural and visual potency
of the play's individual moments easily secures. Thus it is
churlish to be irritated by the unearthing of some of the
discrepancies in a play which is certainly consistent in
respect of its intellectual fascination and emotional power.
Different kinds of dramatic experience, different ways of
seeing and interpreting the world, different conceptions of
characterisation, different themes, different conventions,
different ways of using language slip in and out of focus in
The Merchant of Venice. Here Shakespeare's vision is
multifaceted, protean, magnanimous and fecund, but not
free of the discrepancies to which its creative excesses give
rise. Such creativity proves resistant to selection, the most
negative but also a necessary part of the writer's activity.
The play of mind envinced in *The Merchant of Venice* never
quite succeeds in converging its discrepant materials into
complex coherence. Hence unified readings of the play as
opposed as those of John Russell Brown and A. D. Moody
are unsatisfactory, not because they misinterpret the text,
but because in the interests of that coherence they
necessarily suppress some elements of the play which we
find not merely discrepant but rich in intelligence and
insight. *The Merchant of Venice* deserves more tact and
tentativeness than its defenders habitually accord it.

While that failure in *The Merchant of Venice* to attain to a
full coherence is the play's limitation, we do not do full
justice to the play if we are too ready to invoke that
explanation of many of the play's challenges. For the play is
much more than a mere aggregation of unrelated parts, and
we have seen enough of the play's interrelatednesses by now
to realise that its limitation is a matter of degree. *Many* of the
play's juxtapositions of scene, action, and character are

securely and pointedly present and *much*, though not all, of its discrepancy is cultivated to ironic ends. Moreover, that ultimate failure of unity has compensations locally in the play's exploitation of suddenness and surprise. And the most justly memorable of the play's extreme moments is its trial.

·6·
The Trial

Of itself, the trial scene more than justifies the greatness of *The Merchant of Venice*: it is one of the most astonishing moments in our dramatic history. But typically it requires some fairly clumsy massaging of his story-materials for Shakespeare to bring about the precise circumstances in which the trial is conducted. Since the Venetians are not the most pedantically principled of people, the court must be given sufficiently credible reasons for its paralysed sense of the justice of Shylock's suit. These 'reasons' are dropped rather suddenly into the play in the course of Act 3, and take the form of a little lesson in the law from Antonio:

> The Duke cannot deny the course of law;
> For the commodity that strangers have
> With us in Venice, if it be denied,
> Will much impeach the justice of the state,
> Since that the trade and profit of the city
> Consisteth of all nations.
>
> (III.iii. 26–31)

The origins of Portia's resolution of this legal problem are no less cumbersome. Portia comes to the rescue in the place of the great lawyer, Bellario. But the circumstances of Bellario's unseen role in the plot do not bear much looking into. (Critics bent on the ironic undermining of Portia will find much that is discrepant and contrived in Portia's eagerness to serve as Bellario's replacement, though not to my mind tellingly so.) A great deal of hurried plotting both on and off stage reveals Bellario to be no more than a device to provide Portia with a letter of introduction to the Venetian court and a source for the few legal tricks which the 'unlesson'd girl' will deploy there. And later, Bellario's letter will again come in too handy as an economical means of tying up the confusions which the ring plot has caused. Further scrutiny yields oddities: it is a 'happy' coincidence that Bellario should be both Portia's cousin and the learned doctor for whom the Duke has sent; it is a less 'happy' coincidence that he is, or is supposed to be, sick—thinking practically, Antonio might feel better defended by an expert than by a precocious girl in masculine garb whose pleasure in her concealment may too readily distract her with opportunities to tease her new husband! But such nonchalantly implausible inventiveness is the price the play willingly pays for its own dramatic good fortune.

Shakespeare favours precariousness particularly in the central scenes and in the endings of his plays and seems little interested in observing any proprieties of genre: talk of the inevitability of tragedy or the security of comic resolution does not come readily in discussing Shakespeare. The most familiar examples are perhaps the eruption of death into the romantic resolution of *Love's Labours Lost* and the much-remarked grotesque comedy of *King Lear* but, nearer in time of composition to *The Merchant of Venice*, *Romeo and Juliet*, in the misunderstandings, mistakings and mistimings of its tomb scene, verges on comedy, if not on farce.

It is the trial scene which most substantiates the general feeling with regard to *The Merchant of Venice* representatively described by Alexander Leggatt: 'the physical threat to Antonio, and the intensity of Shylock's emotions, break the immunity, the detachment from real suffering on which comedy normally depends' (Leggatt

1974, p. 119). Yet critics intent on the vilification or the vindication of Shylock emphasise one or other of these claims to seriousness: the threat to Antonio *or* Shylock's pain. On the contrary, the distinctive force of the scene rests not in one or other extremity but in the coupling of the two so that the abrupt reversal in the focal point of the play's crisis forces the emotional intensity of our reaction to double back on itself. The scene brings about a violent dislocation in the attitudes and allegiances it has first worked so hard to provoke, and we find ourselves in the unpleasant and disorientating situation where our response seems to be running counter to itself. The giddiness of Portia's and Bassanio's love scene, which provoked wonder, is here translated into an altogether more unpleasant form of giddiness.

Given the tension and suspense which characterise this scene's effect, we need to attend particularly to the *sequence* of action and argument. In the early moments of the trial, Antonio's danger and Shylock's intransigence are intensified in a sequence of tellings and showings which promotes an escalating sense of urgency and anxiety. The initial description of the crisis comes from the Duke, the most authoritative and powerful figure in the play. His pity for Antonio is mixed with feelings of impotence and frustration:

> I am sorry for thee; thou art come to answer
> A stony adversary, an inhuman wretch,
> Uncapable of pity, void and empty
> From any dram of mercy.
>
> (IV.i. 3–6)

This is substantiated and reinforced by Antonio's reply from which we infer that the Duke has been speaking with the voice of much fruitless effort expended prior to this final hour:

> I have heard
> Your Grace hath ta'en great pains to qualify
> His rigorous course; but since he stands obdurate,
> And that no lawful means carry me
> Out of his envy's reach, I do oppose
> My patience to his fury, and am arm'd
> To suffer with a quietness of spirit
> The very tyranny and rage of his.
>
> (IV.i. 6–13)

What we are told is now confirmed by what we see. On Shylock's appearance, the Duke projects on the occasion a hypothetical and detailed account of future events, a projection of exactly what a first-night audience, new to the play, might hope for:

> Shylock, the world thinks, and I think so too,
> That thou but leads this fashion of thy malice
> To the last hour of act; and then, 'tis thought,
> Thou'lt show thy mercy and remorse, more strange
> Than is thy strange apparent cruelty;
> And where thou now exacts the penalty,
> Which is a pound of this poor merchant's flesh,
> Thou wilt not only loose the forfeiture,
> But, touch'd with human gentleness and love,
> Forgive a moiety óf the principal,
> Glancing an eye of pity on his losses . . .
>
> (IV.i. 17–27)

It is a possibility fulsomely raised only to be denied, even if we feel that the unthinking insult which concludes this lengthy appeal from the Duke—'We all expect a gentle answer, Jew'—contributes further and typically to Shylock's obduracy. The play is at overt and precise pains to narrow the audience's sense of the possible outcomes of the situation before us, and, in this, the dramatist's prolonged and meticulous reiteration does not appear contrived since it is in keeping with the precision and formality of the judicial setting.

In reply to the Duke, Shylock is deliberately aggressive and offensive, first irritated by the need for yet more public confirmation of his unyielding intention, and then threatening the Duke with a reminder of the general danger to the city's freedom and charter of any averting of the course of justice in this particular case. Shylock's frightening power is again evident in the way that he can anticipate and control both sides of a conversation, and in the way he aggressively reduces the world around him to the most basic and physical. He is unanswerable and untouchable because his direct and reductive honesty explicitly declares the irrationality and pointlessness of his behaviour. His words are an unyielding and invulnerable refusal of accommodation. And ironically Shylock's voice has now found its true home, not in human society, but in the courtroom which is the symptom of human society's imperfections.

Prior to taking physical revenge on Antonio, Shylock exacts a more general revenge on the Venetians in a pedantically laboured account of human behaviour where humanity is stripped of its dignity and reduced to irrational mechanism. And the Venetians are obliged to listen. The justice of Shylock's legal claim forces upon the court a tolerance of the Jew's intolerance. The Venetians' interventions are little more than exclamations of frustration, revealing their true nature in the ill-controlled violence of Gratiano's abusive raillery.

Antonio's emphatic interruption of Bassanio's futile challenging of Shylock writes the violence, animalism and heartlessness of Shylock in large elemental terms, and underlines the irony that the Christians' feeble but well-intentioned procrastination may not be a kindness to Shylock's victim. It illuminates, too, the dilemma later revealed to confront the Duke in deciding whether or not to postpone the trial until Bellario's arrival. Bassanio is forced back from moral and human argument into an attempt to buy Shylock off, only for the Jew to parody the confidence which Portia had earlier expressed in the power of inflated offers:

> Bassanio   For thy three thousand ducats here is six.
> Shylock   If every ducat in six thousand ducats
>   Were in six parts, and every part a ducat,
>   I would not draw them; I would have my
>   bond.
>
>   (IV.i. 84–7)

In this scene Shakespeare's manipulation of his audience into a state of anxious suspense is perhaps of a kind we more readily associate with lesser art. However, the simplicity of the dramatic method accords with the primitivism it exposes, and the greater seriousness here derives from our sense of the greater seriousness of the issues and the greater substance of the characters involved. Shakespeare teases his audience with the arrival of Portia, heralded by Bellario's confidently optimistic letter, but the hope is raised only to be dashed as confidence transforms itself into something less comforting—the legalistic coolness of Portia's conduct, playing up, as she is, to her role as Doctor of Laws. We are troubled in a second way by Portia's cool disinterestedness. This is pointed by the scene but unperceived by the characters on stage. For there is a second contest beyond the opposition of Antonio and Shylock, lurking here in the rival claims of Antonio and Portia on Bassanio, and Portia's attitude of professional detachment may appear to be an unsympathetic underestimating of Antonio's value and love. The tensions which will sustain the ring plot emerge here in asides, as Bassanio's declaration for Antonio is comically parodied by Gratiano but returned, in Shylock's unfinished musings, to a deeper suggestion of the irresolvable conflicts in the loyalties of love:

Bassanio	Antonio, I am married to a wife
	Which is as dear to me as life itself;
	But life itself, my wife, and all the world,
	Are not with me esteem'd above thy life;
	I would lose all, ay, sacrifice them all
	Here to this devil, to deliver you.
Portia	Your wife would give you little thanks for
	that,
	If she were by to hear you make the offer.
Gratiano	I have a wife who I protest I love;
	I would she were in heaven, so she could
	Entreat some power to change this currish
	Jew.
Nerissa	'Tis well you offer it behind her back;
	The wish would make else an unquiet
	house.
Shylock [Aside]	These be the Christian husbands! I
	have a daughter—
	Would any of the stock of Barrabas
	Had been her husband, rather than a
	Christian!—
	We trifle time; I pray thee pursue sentence.

(IV.i. 277–93)

But such trifles will worry us again in the final Act of the play.

In the courtroom, the full scale of Shylock's intransigence is reiterated for us in Portia's long-drawn-out cross-examination, and the physicality of Shylock's language now spills over into the visually forceful physicality of action as the knife is whetted and Antonio's chest laid bare for it: events have come to a point of crisis beyond comedy.

But Portia's coldness is also scrupulousness. To lament, as A. D. Moody does, that 'Portia is all along preparing to smite in sunder the loins of the unmerciful' (Moody 1964, p. 42) is to judge Portia and the scene retrospectively. Goddard is even more damning:

What possessed Portia to torture not only Antonio but her own husband with such superfluous suspense? She knew what was coming. Why didn't she let it come at once? Why didn't she invoke immediately the law prescribing a penalty for any alien plotting against the life of any citizen of Venice instead of waiting until she had put those she supposedly loved upon the rack? The only possible answer is that she wanted a spectacle, a dramatic triumph with herself at the center.

(Goddard 1960, p. 109)

But we, Shakespeare's audience, are by no means as immune from the dramatic spectacle as such analysis supposes since, as we watch, we do *not* know what is coming. Even with hindsight, Portia's 'torture' may not be 'superfluous'. With an opponent as legalistically precise as Shylock, Portia needs as much public evidence of the reality of Shylock's malevolent intent as he can be brought to give, and it is perhaps only *at* the last moment that the last-moment solution can be safely and effectively revealed.

I'm not sure how convinced I am by my last suggestion above. It smacks a little of the academic's attempt to close the troublesome gap in *The Merchant of Venice* between our immediate sense of what we see happening before us and the speculations which we pursue *after* the drama has been played out. *The Merchant of Venice* is no mere piece of theatrical ephemera: the play is of a substance to merit and require the kinds of sustained recollection and speculation which occur subsequent to our enjoyment of the play in the theatre. Certainly, Portia suffers when considered with hindsight. Her behaviour both here in the trial scene and in the earlier love scene loses its initial attractiveness, and the more we remember and ponder it, the more mixed its motives can appear. How much looking into can Portia's actions bear? And how close a scrutiny of Portia's actions is it *appropriate* for us to make? We are encountering again the same kinds of difficulty over the limits of plausible interpretation which we felt with regard to Lorenzo and Jessica. Are we scrutinising a shallow and less than thoroughly agreeable character? Or are we worrying too much over an example of characterisation limited deliberately by the dramatist because his interests and emphases lie elsewhere? Is our concern with Portia a distraction from, or a deepening of our awareness of what is really at issue in *The Merchant of Venice*? Both the degree and kind of attention which the different characters ask of us at different moments in the play seem extraordinarily uncertain and ever-changing. And the portrayal of Portia, most of all, exemplifies that changeability of emphasis and treatment. If Shylock is the play's strongest and most discussed piece of characterisation, then Portia is its most perplexing for interpretation.

Bound up with our uncertainties over Portia is a further uncertainty: where is the great central scene in *The Merchant of Venice*? Is it Portia's and Bassanio's love scene, or is it the thwarting of Shylock here in the Venetian courtroom? It would be foolish to deny *any* play more than one great and central moment. But in the particular case of *The Merchant of Venice*, as we are discovering, the two climactic moments—Bassanio's winning of Portia, and the defeat of Shylock—seem to be rivals for more than our attention and admiration. These two scenes are at odds with each other in prompting two opposed and irreconcilable ways of regarding *The Merchant of Venice*. Certainly, as Shylock's suffering is now displayed before us, it proves increasingly difficult to sustain the broadly favourable view of Portia, and of the Christians generally, which we had held prior to the trial.

When the reversal of fortunes comes in this scene, and the trial of Shylock is subsequently given a dramatic elaboration no less prolonged than the trial of Antonio which preceded it, it brings with it a momentum of relief which carries the audience in acquiescence with the action beyond the point where we find, retrospectively, that we can condone it. Our embarrassment first registers itself in response to the excited interjections of Gratiano, and subsequently in response to the more far-reaching actions of Portia and the court, over which the play lingers more than we increasingly might wish.

The source of our discomfort is quite simple: a character we have identified as villainous because of his attitudes and arguments, and because he evinces a want of human sympathy, is defeated by the same kind of arguments and subjected to attitudes similarly devoid of sympathy. The Christians out-Shylock Shylock as the letter of the law defeats the letter of the law in ways oblivious to its spirit and destructive of the human spirit. There is a hideous appropriateness in the justice meted out to Shylock: the parallels between the treatment he sought to visit on Antonio and the treatment he now receives are strikingly precise. Indeed, the irritatingly loquacious Gratiano need look no further than the repetition of Shylock's own words for his unfeeling 'wit':

O Jew! an upright judge, a learned judge!

A second Daniel, a Daniel, Jew!
Now, infidel, I have you on the hip.

A Daniel still say I, a second Daniel!
I thank thee, Jew, for teaching me that word.

(IV.I. 318, 328–9, 335–6)

The Christians' actions indirectly deprive Shylock of his life no less surely than Shylock's claiming of his pound of flesh would have destroyed Antonio:

Shylock   Nay, take my life and all, pardon not that.
           You take my house when you do take the
           prop

That doth sustain my house; you take my
        life
When you do take the means whereby I
        live.

(IV.i. 369–72)

The kindness which Antonio is now prepared to offer
Shylock is no less cruel than the kindness which, at the
beginning of the play, Shylock had shown the merchant.
Lorenzo's theft of Jessica arguably prompted Shylock to the
extremity of his revenge, and now, at Antonio's request, all
that remains in Shylock's possession is to be willed to the
'gentleman' thief. Shylock's justification of his actions—
inasmuch as he had one—had been that he was merely
emulating the Christians: 'The villainy you teach me I will
execute'. Now the Christians' revenge betters Shylock's
instruction to the extent that he is not merely allowed to
emulate the Christians but is forced to become one. (The
argument that Elizabethan audiences might regard
Shylock's conversion as a fortunate means of saving his soul
is contextually fatuous. While Shylock sought to destroy
Antonio physically, these Christians are here bent on
destroying Shylock's spirit.) The disquieting symmetry is
completed when Shylock is forced into the agreement of a
bond no more merry than the original one he had made with
Antonio:

Duke   He shall do this, or else I do recant
            The pardon that I late pronounced here.
Portia   Art thou contented, Jew? What dost thou
                    say?
Shylock   I am content.
Portia   Clerk, draw a deed of gift.
Shylock   I pray you, give me leave to go from hence;
            I am not well; send the deed after me
            And I will sign it.

(IV.i. 388–92)

This community preserves itself by violation of the values to which it lays claim, and by the same means as those deployed by the alien who threatens it. Its prejudices blind it to the damning identity underlying the ostensible opposition.

Just as some critics seem *too quick* to take offence at Portia, other readings of the trial scene contrive to sustain an altogether more favourable view of the Christians. It is important that such views be represented here, although it seems to me that they often sustain their attitude by way of an inattention to the particulars of the latter part of the scene, and that, when confronting the details of the sentence passed on Shylock, they appear perverse or unintelligible by turns. John Russell Brown concedes that these Christians are not without their imperfections but invokes Shylock's fate in a manner which virtually makes the Jew's mistreatment his own fault, and thus Brown manages finally to maintain his balance with the sacrifice of only Gratiano:

> It is Shylock's fate to bring out the worst in those he tries to harm: the 'good Antonio' shows unfeeling contempt towards him, the light-hearted Salerio and Solanio become wantonly malicious when they meet him, and Portia, once she has turned the trial against him, wounds him still further with sarcastic humour. The trial scene shows that the pursuit of love's wealth does not necessarily bring with it a universal charity, a love which reaches even to one's enemies. The balance is fairly kept, for Antonio and the Duke magnanimously spare Shylock's life and this is thrown into relief by the irresponsible malice of Gratiano.
>
> (Brown 1962, p. 174)

Sigurd Burckhardt argues, with a logic which escapes me, that Shylock's punishment is indeed Shylock's responsibility and fault, and at times *sounds as if* he is castigating Shylock for failing to kill Antonio:

If we read Portia's judgment as a legal trick and Shylock's defeat as a foregone conclusion, the Jew's final humiliation must appear distressingly cruel. But there is good reason for reading the scene differently. Portia's ruling is one more hazard, and Shylock's moral collapse does not demolish the bond and all it stands for, but rather proves him unequal to the faith he has professed. Even after the judgment the issue is in doubt; it is still in Shylock's power to turn the play into a tragedy, to enforce the letter of the bond and to take the consequences. But at this point and before this choice he breaks, turns apostate to the faith he has so triumphantly forced upon his enemies. Having made the gentles bow before the letter of the law, he is now asked to become, literally, a blood witness. But he reneges and surrenders the bond's power, and like a renegade he is flogged into gentleness.

(Burckhardt, in Wilders 1969, p. 221)

The concluding schoolmasterly contortion is bizarre indeed.

There is a sadism, too, in the way Portia insists on the ceremonial formalities of the trial to its very end, and in her choice of contentment as the form which Shylock's agreement has to take she secures both the appearance of righteous vindication for herself and the humiliating denial of Shylock's dignity. Shylock is forced back to muttered assent, laconic excuse and finally the panicked silence of his exit:

Duke   Get thee gone, but do it.
Gratiano In christ'ning shalt thou have two god-
                    fathers;
                    Had I been judge, thou shouldst have had
                       ten more,

To bring thee to the gallows, not to the
        font.

Exit Shylock.
(IV.i. 392–5)

I think the feeling which dominates this moment in the play
is shame. The full effect on an audience of Shylock's hurried
and silent exit can be gauged only if we measure it against the
expectations which the rest of the play has generated.
Entrances and exits throughout *The Merchant of Venice* have
been marked by a certain formality, and thus the dramatic
incongruousness of Shylock's being deprived of an exit line
is all the more awkward. In *Twelfth Night* Malvolio's 'I'll be
reveng'd on the whole pack of you' (V.i. 364) is anything but
serene, but he at least is allowed the dignity of a last word;
Shylock is denied even that.

It is difficult to see how the play might recover its
equilibrium after that exit. It manages what is at best a
diversion. Because of the formality of the court setting and
because of Portia's disguise, the trial scene is without that
revealing naturalism of dialogue which we have remarked
elsewhere in the play. In the latter stages of the trial only
Gratiano has been voluble in expressing how he feels about
what is happening; the others, we might infer, are wise
enough to keep silent. The events of the trial scene are never
directly discussed retropectively, and Shylock, barely
alluded to, is never again mentioned for his own sake.

The abruptness with which the subject is changed after
Shylock's exit comes as a relief for these characters. And the
speed with which the Duke leaves the stage with his train
after a perfunctory invitation and a sparse and oblique
reference to the means by which Antonio's deliverance was
effected, suggests that the Duke would much rather be
elsewhere. If there is to be the celebration which often
attends on comedy, it is not here and not now.

The characters' embarrassed reticence is also the
dramatist's, and in the succeeding action the play can only

afford embarrassed glances at its own troublesomeness. The oil-and-water nature of this drama finally cannot bring the valuable things we have seen in the Portia whom Bassanio wins and the Portia, albeit the disguised Portia, we have just seen within a single coherent character. The discrepancies reflect not merely human nature but a failure of artistic unity. Consistency is sacrificed to controversy. If we, Shakespeare's audience, are to 'stay with' the play, then we too need to cultivate a relieved forgetfulness. Ostensibly praising the playwright's theatrical skill, Harley Granville-Barker betrays such a need: 'The action must sweep ahead and no chance be given us to question its likelihood. . . . The less we look back upon it, the sooner we come to fresh comedy again the better' (Granville-Barker 1958, Vol. 1, p. 351).

The play's incidental but by no means meagre gain from an inclusiveness in excess of coherence is the abruptly shocking reversal of a scene quite unlike any other in the Shakespearean *oeuvre*. But elsewhere in that *oeuvre* Shakespeare will make use of the insights and methods of the trial scene and will integrate these more securely with the broader development of the plays in which they occur. If there are different Portias present in *The Merchant of Venice*, there are different Shylocks too, each provoking a different kind of reaction in the audience. In the scenes of which he is the centre Shylock is a character of increasing psychological interest and human depth. In the scenes where he is peripheral, or absent yet important and mentioned, he remains a stock villain, a piece of characterisation subordinate to other dramatic emphases. Hence the fudging in what, if we look too hard, is Jessica's lie to Portia in Belmont (III.ii. 286–92) about the longstanding determination of her father's malevolent intentions, and the fudging in the contrived single appearance of Tubal. While, in *The Merchant of Venice*, we see the beginnings of a larger control over the sequence of Shylocks exposed to our view so that the troublingly human claims he makes on an audience intensify in his later appearances, that control is more securely and demonstrably present in the case of Shakespeare's portrayal of Malvolio in *Twelfth Night*. Malvolio is a lesser figure than Shylock and, confined to the comic subplot of *Twelfth Night*, his threat is the lesser. But from Malvolio's encroachment on Sir Toby's and Sir Andrew's revels, through the first moments of his deception—which Malvolio himself enjoys—to his wantonly tortured confinement and subsequent public humiliation at the play's close, we are, as it were, moved steadily and coherently through ninety degrees in our view of *both* Malvolio *and* those who first seem oppressed by him and who gradually reveal themselves as his persecutors. Such an effect is what Shakespeare seems to reach for, but never quite secures in *The Merchant of Venice*. But perhaps, conversely, *Twelfth Night*'s dynamic coherence forfeits the sudden discomfort of Shylock's trial.

In the trial scene of *The Merchant of Venice* Shakespeare discovers in the medium of legal argument and in the debate over justice and mercy, an effective context which brings definition to his exploration of what I have characterised as the tensions between accommodation and principle. But here the opportunity is not fully taken. The argument over justice and mercy is embarked upon, but is then dropped to be replaced by arguments which are all justice, and justice of an implausibly tricksy kind. For all its eloquence, Portia's famous speech about mercy finally proves irrelevant to the resolution of this particular dilemma. And this Portia herself seems to recognise almost as she speaks it:

> I have spoke thus much
> To mitigate the justice of thy plea,
> Which if thou follow, this strict court of Venice
> Must needs give sentence 'gainst the merchant there.
> (IV.i. 197–200)

While the subsequent disregarding of mercy by those who

advocate it reflects badly on Portia and the Christians—'It is a good divine that follows his own instructions'—it suggests, too, that the dramatist himself cannot at this time take the more interestingly involved debate any further. An absolute insistence on justice can entail a denial of human feeling and human dignity, such as we are to see here. But mercy can prove difficult to distinguish from irresponsible licence, and it too can entail a devaluing of human life and meaning, and a loosening of the bonds which make for social dignity. Both Portia, here, and Isabella in *Measure for Measure*, in citing the divine precedent for mercy, fail to see the vulnerability of their position. They do not recognise that the remedy they advocate may entail the payment of a painful price, a price which Christ himself paid with his own sacrifice:

> *Portia*   But mercy is above this sceptred sway,
> It is enthroned in the hearts of kings,
> It is an attribute to God himself;
> And earthly power doth then show likest
>   God's
> When mercy seasons justice. Therefore, Jew,
> Though justice be thy plea, consider this—
> That in the course of justice none of us
> Should see salvation; we do pray for mercy,
> And that same prayer doth teach us all to
>   render
> The deeds of mercy.
>   (IV.i. 188–97)

> *Isabella*   Why, all the souls that were were forfeit
>   once;
> And He that might the vantage best have
>   took
> Found out the remedy. How would you be
> If He, which is the top of judgment, should
> But judge you as you are? O, think on that;

And mercy then will breathe within your
    lips,
Like man new made.
            (*Measure for Measure* II.ii. 73–9)

In *The Merchant of Venice* these problems are again touched
on when Bassanio characteristically advocates, not mercy
precisely, but a mitigation of justice and the law:

Bassanio   And, I beseech you,
        Wrest once the law to your authority;
        To do a great right do a little wrong,
        And curb this cruel devil of his will.
Portia   It must not be; there is no power in Venice
        Can alter a decree established;
        'Twill be recorded for a precedent,
        And many an error, by the same example,
        Will rush into the state; it cannot be.
            (IV.i. 209–17)

This too finds its way into *Measure for Measure*, not merely
as a local argument but as an idea which shapes the
developing action and plot:

Isabella   Yet show some pity.
Angelo   I show it most of all when I show justice;
        For then I pity those I do not know,
        Which a dismiss'd offence would after gall,
        And do him right that, answering one foul
           wrong,
        Lives not to act another.
        (*Measure for Measure* II.ii. 99–104)

As the plot unfolds, Isabella will discover herself in the
position of destined victim of the precise crime for which
she here urges mercy. Angelo will find himself guilty of the
same crime as the man on whom he visits unyielding justice.

In *Measure for Measure* dramatic action is a germane challenge to the adequacy of argument.

The development in *The Merchant of Venice* is less focused and more tangential. The complex issues outlined above slip from the play to be replaced by something simpler, the cruel hypocrisy of Portia's excessive justice. I suggest that in the trial scene of *The Merchant of Venice* the urgencies of the particular case overwhelm our potential attentiveness to complex general argument, and we notice this example of the stringent legality of man's double inhumanity to man more than the niceties of the arguments which accompany it. In *Measure for Measure* the exploration of mercy and justice which surfaces briefly in the trial scene of *The Merchant of Venice* now shapes a much larger part of the play. The particular law at issue, while perhaps no less idiosyncratic and harsh, is now single and simple. The play more successfully controls the attention we pay to both general issue and particular case—that of Claudio and Juliet—so that the challenging problem of their interrelatedness is brought into focus. The characters themselves now perceive more of the complex relationship between the general problem and the particular life on trial. In some ways, then, the exploratory and energetic creativity of *The Merchant of Venice* bears its fullest individual fruits beyond the individual play.

· 7 ·

Rings and Echoes

It is a very odd play that gets a new and independent plot fully under way only its last Act. The oddity is compounded by the way in which the ring plot teases us with echoes of what has preceded it, but echoes only half-heard since they seem to resist specificity and pointedness. Events at the end of the play set us thinking about the play's relatednesses but withhold the more precise elaborations which might give a fuller substantiality to our speculations. The degree to which individual spectators and readers are provoked by such elusive echoes will vary, I suggest, with the degree to which they have been unsettled by the actions which have preceded these intrigues in Belmont.

Most obviously, Bassanio is not the first character in this play to be distressed by a ring's entangling of one's loyalties and loves:

> Tubal   One of them showed me a ring that he had of
>   your daughter for a monkey.
> Shylock Out upon her! Thou torturest me, Tubal. It
>   was my turquoise; I had it of Leah when I was a
>   bachelor; I would not have given it for a
>   wilderness of monkeys.
>
>   (III.i. 101–6)

But, assuming that we do register the parallel, what further direction are our thoughts given? The tangential ring plot appears to contain, not a development, but a niggling residue of the play's earlier concerns. Underlying its immediate pleasures, there appear to be conflicting intentions at work, none fully and unequivocally realised.

The last scene offers itself variously as a lyrical celebration of love, harmony and community, a lively and bawdy comedy of sexual confusions, and an ironic undermining of Belmont's lovers. And, with varying degrees of knowingness, it falls short of all such possibilities. A wistful sadness tinges the lyricism; the light comedy hints at darker underlying seriousnesses; the bawdy can become jarringly tactless; and the ironic suggestions hold back from any directed precision. Perhaps we have heard too much of the open text, but Shakespeare is habitually drawn to endings which work on different levels and in different directions. He is too resourceful a dramatist not to succeed in drawing his story material into some kind of resolution, and too intelligent a thinker to resist the further opportunities for interrogative and subversive scepticism. *Measure for Measure*, in this as in so many respects *The Merchant of Venice*'s sister play, contrives a resolution of the various dilemmas of its plot, which works if we don't look too hard but which, in the self-advertising improbabilities of its bedtrick and ducal fumblings, invites equally sharp scrutiny.

But the immediate pleasures of the final scene are not to be slighted. Like the scene in which Bassanio wins Portia, the opening of Act 5 does contain verbal ironies and darknesses, but these are overwhelmed by the larger setting, its music and the eloquent cadences of its poetry. To emphasize subversion and undermining in Jessica's and Lorenzo's exchange is to read them against their grain. A.D.Moody manages to sound at once dismissive of the romantic lumber and churlishly peeved at the play's resistance to his own emphasis:

No one will miss the midsummer's night atmosphere of the last act, with the moon making a second day of the night, the poetry of legendary lovers, and the perfecting of the mood by the music brought forth into the air. This idyll of music, moonlight and love is wholly removed from the trial and from everything to do with Shylock, and seems to offer the apotheosis of the love of Venice and Belmont. However, we will find, if our wits are not dreaming, that we are in the same world as before, beneath the moon in fortune's world of 'will' and fickle chance. There is some passing talk of heavenly harmony, but the last word is Gratiano's, and it resolves the teasing business of the rings and broken vows only in an earthy pun. (Moody 1964, pp.44–5)

But such talk is not so easily passed over. Certainly, underlying the patterned love dialogue of Lorenzo and Jessica—'In such a night'—there is a less harmonious exchange of reproach and threatened betrayals (see Berry 1985, pp. 59–61). But it is conducted obliquely by means of a witty rivalry of allusion to the betrayed and unfortunate lovers of classical myth—Troilus and Cressida, Thisby, Dido, Medea. And even these allusions to past tragedies and duplicities are further muted since Shakespeare's immediate sources seem to be, not the stark world of classical tragedy, but Chaucer and, in the case of Thisby, his own comedy *A Midsummer Night's Dream*. If there is a darker realism here continuous with our earlier sense of the imperfections of Lorenzo and Jessica and with the glimpsed imbalance in their relationship, then it is displaced to the very periphery of a scene where stylised dialogue numbs thought as it increases our pleasure. The *kind* of attention we pay to what is being said is controlled by tone, rhythm, rhyme and by a rich musicality of assonance and alliteration. These characters are magnanimously allowed a moment of fineness in excess of their characteristic selves and there is a melancholy self-consciousness in the play which recognises this, and recognises the means by which it is secured. Thus the special nature of the moment allows Lorenzo a philosophical far-sightedness which, dispassionately regarded, is far in advance of his normal powers:

> Here will we sit and let the sounds of music
> Creep in our ears; soft stillness and the night
> Become the touches of sweet harmony.
> . . .
> Such harmony is in immortal souls,
> But while this muddy vesture of decay
> Doth grossly close it in, we cannot hear it.
>
> (V.i. 55–65)

In reply to Jessica's sadly wondering 'I am never merry when I hear sweet music', Lorenzo expounds on the transforming power of music in ways which entail an oblique reference to the contrastingly unmusical Shylock, the man who has no time for the 'shallow fopp'ry' of fife and drum:

> . . . nought so stockish, hard, and full of rage,
> But music for the time doth change his nature.
> The man that hath no music in himself,
> Nor is not mov'd with concord of sweet sounds,
> Is fit for treasons, stratagems, and spoils;
> The motions of his spirit are dull as night,
> And his affections dark as Erebus.
> Let no such man be trusted. Mark the music.
>
> (V.i. 81–8)

Whatever our misgivings at earlier mistreatments of Shylock, we do mark the music here. Artistic transformation may also be artful deceit, but in the moments of its playing it is not something which we wish to resist. Typically, it is in retrospect, and away from the immediate context, that Lorenzo and Jessica, and our complicity in their pleasure, again become troubling. No less than our hostility to Shylock, our indulgence of his opponents can prove a source of embarrassment.

With the arrival of Portia the play becomes even more wistfully remote from the specifics of its own action. The philosophical generalities here come as a relief from the pressing particularities of the trial. What Portia's disquisition recognises is the gap between the ideal and the actual, between the absolute and the possible. She goes on to recognise that morality is relative: our sense of good depends on what it is judged against, and on our perspective in judging it. Such speculation has a teasingly elusive relation to the events of the play, and to Portia's own actions, but a relation more easily sensed than specified:

Enter Portia and Nerissa.

Portia   That light we see is burning in my hall.
           How far that little candle throws his beams!
           So shines a good deed in a naughty world.

Nerissa   When the moon shone, we did not see the
           candle.

Portia   So doth the greater glory dim the less:
           A substitute shines brightly as a king
           Until a king be by, and then his state
           Empties. itself, as doth an inland brook
           Into the main of waters. Music! hark!

Nerissa   It is your music, madam, of the house.

Portia   Nothing is good, I see, without respect;
           Methinks it sounds much sweeter than by
           day.

Nerissa   Silence bestows that virtue on it, madam.

Portia   The crow doth sing as sweetly as the lark
           When neither is attended; and I think
           The nightingale, if she should sing by day,
           When every goose is cackling, would be
               thought
           No better a musician than the wren.

How many things by season season'd are
To their right praise and true perfection!
(V.i. 89–108)

Such eloquence is curiously and seductively moving, but sententiousness, even as elegiacally accepting as this is, remains in a problematic relation to the dramatic action. The words derive their mournful authority from Portia's voice of experience, but our sense of the ways in which they refer to such past experiences remains hazy. The larger particularities of this play seem curiously to slip between the immediate and mundane incidentals which prompt Portia's musings—the candle in her own house, the overhearing of her own music—and the conceited elaborations which her thoughts receive. We might suspect that Portia's wisdom is in fact the dramatist's sleight of hand, and that what matters here is mood, not philosophy. We are being seduced into acquiescence with a course of action which had caused us disquiet, and our troubled sense of characters who had proved all too human is being converted to an acceptance of their fallible—and therefore reassuring—humanity. Our unease is soothed into accommodation but, as Alexander Leggatt notes, Portia's lofty moment 'achieves its confidence only by keeping off the problems of the characters themselves' (Leggatt 1974, p. 146). But the dramatic action cannot be arrested in such elevated quietism for long: Bassanio and Gratiano are also returning to Belmont.

How seriously do we take Bassanio's misplaced ring? Viewed simply as an artefact, the ring represents a diverting comedy of temporary misunderstanding easily resolved by its restoration in the revelation that Portia and the young Doctor of Laws are one and the same. Viewed symbolically, the ring exposes a division of loyalties, a failure of absolute fidelity and a tension between different obligations and bonds. The characters fail to perceive the full scale of such problems and they resolve their difficulties too easily and cheaply in a neat trick. Typically, the play wavers between these two possibilities.

Earlier in the play, Bassanio having left Belmont to attend to the threatened Antonio, Portia plays out the curious scene of her own planned departure (III.iv). It begins in high seriousness as Lorenzo eulogises Bassanio and Antonio to be answered by a similarly solemn recognition, on Portia's part, of the 'hellish cruelty' of the situation in Venice. But then Portia moves incongruously to merry plotting and contrivance as she anticipates, with Nerissa, jolly marital japes in Venice. Husbands are to be encountered unawares as the two women 'accomplished/ With what [they] lack' outdo each other in youthful swagger, martial bravado and bragging fictions of the 'honourable ladies' who have swooned in their paths. As it turns out, the trial affords no such opportunity for the sexual play, innuendo and affected swagger which excite Portia and Nerissa here. Portia's sombre disguise as a Doctor of Laws transforms her profession and only incidentally her gender. The seriousness of the trial cannot accommodate the sexual comedy of disguise which therefore gets displaced beyond the immediate occasion of Portia's transformation to the coda of the ring plot. Yet the exchange of rings never fully frees itself from the circumstances of the trial but remains *both* an entertaining relief from those urgent events *and* a disconcerting prolongation of the same concerns. Antonio is the overlapping centre of both actions.

This uncertainty is reflected in the doubleness of events in Venice immediately after the trial. Portia's initial request of the ring is taken very seriously by Bassanio, who is now at odds with himself and his obligations. He shifts uneasily between the evasive excuse that the ring is 'a trifle' and the opposite admission that 'There's more depends on this than on the value'. In fact, Bassanio passes Portia's test, and it is only *after* the departure of the young Doctor of Laws that Antonio makes his uncharacteristically self-assertive intervention:

> My Lord Bassanio, let him have the ring,
> Let his deservings, and my love withal,
> Be valued 'gainst your wife's commandment.
>
> (IV.i. 444–6)

This is the most that Antonio ever asks of Bassanio, and it is a poignant and solemn moment. But what is surprising is that Portia, in the subsequent scene where she receives the ring, is neither disconcerted by Bassanio's change of mind nor curious about the circumstances—unknown to her—in which her husband broke his pledge. Her exchanges with Nerissa, anticipating discomfited husbands in Belmont, register none of the seriousness of potential conflict which Antonio's directness had brought momentarily to the surface:

> Nerissa I'll see if I can get my husband's ring,
> Which I did make him swear to keep for
> ever.
> Portia Thou may'st, I warrant. We shall have old
> swearing
> That they did give the rings away to men;
> But we'll outface them, and outswear them
> too.
>
> (IV.ii. 13–17)

There is a slightness about the ensuing business which concludes *The Merchant of Venice*, and we are insulated from any anxieties which might otherwise attend its unfolding by our prior knowledge of how precisely it will resolve itself. With the departure of Shylock, the dramatic texture of the play thins and relaxes from some of its previous tautness. The basic comic situation which now arises in Belmont is obvious and rather ordinary. It is telling that the greater dramatic life in its playing-out should reveal itself in the characters, not of Portia and Bassanio, but of Nerissa and Gratiano. This couple, everywhere else in the play the parodic shadow of Portia and Bassanio, dominate the action here. Theirs are the first and last words on a bawdy intrigue which belongs securely to their more superficial and less subtle world. And Antonio appears as an incongruous refugee from an altogether more inward and serious play.

On Bassanio's return to Belmont, Portia talks obliquely to the air and only latterly directs her greeting to her husband. Her affected humility is in fact setting up Bassanio's vulnerability:

> Let me give light, but let me not be light,
> For a light wife doth make a heavy husband,
> And never be Bassanio so for me;
> But God sort all! You are welcome home, my lord.
>
> (V.i. 129–32)

The sorting out is not to be left to God. The ring is securely in Portia's possession. We recognise the familiar comic situation of marital teasing. But, while we are thus remote from the seriousness of any Shylockian situation, we might momentarily glimpse a Portia no less skilled in the manipulation of dialogue and morality than Shylock, and a Portia officiously akin to the young Doctor of Laws of the trial scene. When the row erupts, not between Portia and Bassanio but between Nerissa and Gratiano, we have two centres of comic interest on stage—the more energetically vociferous reproaches of Gratiano and Nerissa, and the increasingly uneasy silence of Bassanio, Portia's destined victim.

The escalating confusion is orchestrated by Portia, who assumes the role of disinterested adjudicator and deliberately invokes the analogy of Bassanio's assured loyalty:

> You were to blame, I must be plain with you,
> To part so slightly with your wife's first gift,

A thing stuck on with oaths upon your finger
And so riveted with faith unto your flesh.
I gave my love a ring, and made him swear
Never to part with it, and here he stands;
I dare be sworn for him he would not leave it
Nor pluck it from his finger for the wealth
That the world masters. Now, in faith, Gratiano,
You give your wife too unkind a cause of grief;
An 'twere to me, I should be mad at it.
                                        (V.i. 166–76)

After such a schoolmistressy dressing down, the blurting out of Gratiano's excuse is inevitable:

My Lord Bassanio gave his ring away . . .
                                        (V.i. 179)

The reproachful exchanges which ensue reveal the dramatist uncertain whether to show Portia and Bassanio emulating Nerissa and Gratiano in their concentration on the more physical aspects of conjugal rights and duties, or to allow them to pursue the deeper senses of their relationship's emotional obligations and betrayals.

The idiom of these closing moments is nervously unsettled. No single register gets sufficiently under way to establish a predominant idiom from which we might measure departures and gauge their significance. The quibblings of cuckoldry and androgyny—pens to be marred, clerks to be gelded, rings to keep safe, doctors for bedfellows—jostle uneasily against the formal repetitions of more serious talk. Again, the full force of the more sombre declarations is diminished by our sharing in the overplayed joke of concealed identity:

Bassanio   Sweet Portia,
        If you did know to whom I gave the ring,
        If you did know for whom I gave the ring,

> And would conceive for what I gave the
>   ring,
> And how unwillingly I left the ring, . . .
>   (V.i. 192–6)

What Bassanio has to say is moving, but, in context, we don't attend fully to the emotional quality of his words because we know, and Portia knows, all these things in a more mundane and literal way than Bassanio intends. And the trick whereby Portia and the Doctor of Laws are one and the same ensures that the play need never confront Portia's and Bassanio's different views of the obligations of love.

At these moments the play seems too light to bear the weight of its own allusions to its own past actions. But they are there in plenty. Bonds are again at issue. We have already seen that Portia can appear as manipulative as Shylock, and she goes on to 'play' Bassanio as she 'played' Shylock, drawing out Bassanio's trial in a joke which is not without a degree of humiliation. Again, this scene is curiously bloodless and its moments of extreme expression are but the casual metaphors of exaggerated exclamation. But they echo earlier moments of more substantial threat and violence:

>   your wife's first gift,
> A thing stuck on with oaths upon your finger
> And so riveted with faith unto your flesh.
>   (V.i. 167–9)

> Why, I were best to cut my left hand off,
> And swear I lost the ring defending it.
>   (V.i. 177–8)

It is around Antonio, the 'unhappy subject of these quarrels', that these retrospective allusions accumulate, and it is he who, in the midst of the marital banter, gives the parallels an emphasis of alarming solemnity:

I once did lend my body for his wealth,
Which, but for him that had your husband's ring,
Had quite miscarried; I dare be bound again,
My soul upon the forfeit, that your lord
Will never more break faith advisedly.

(V.i. 249–53)

Previously, Antonio risked his flesh and life for Bassanio. Now he is brought to offer something altogether more precious. Antonio may have mistaken the occasion, but his offer calls into question how far Belmont's harmony extends beyond the superficial and how far it depends on something less precarious than tricks, coincidence and contrivance.

There is a perfunctoriness in the play's resolution. We do not see the characters move beyond their initial surprise at Portia's final revelations, the details of which, if lingered over, prove less unequivocally joyous than might appear. Antonio, initially struck dumb by Portia's news of his returned argosies, can only muster a sadly formal thanks:

Sweet lady, you have given me life and living;
For here I read for certain that my ships
Are safely come to road.

(V.i. 286–8)

Isolated in a gathering of couples, the quality of Antonio's projected life and living has an emotional sterility not far removed from the future of a Shylock whose words in the trial Antonio now ostensibly reverses:

Nay, take my life and all, pardon not that.
You take my house when you do take the prop
That doth sustain my house; you take my life
When you do take the means whereby I live.

(IV.i. 369-72)

The brevity of Lorenzo's gratitude for his new windfall
incidentally betrays that that couple's prodigality has
already exhausted what they had stolen from Shylock:

> Fair ladies, you drop manna in the way
> Of starved people.
>
> (V.i. 294–5)

And the play finally narrows to the tawdriness of Gratiano's
last words of sexual anticipation:

> The first inter'gatory
> That my Nerissa shall be sworn on is,
> Whether till the next night she had rather stay,
> Or go to bed now, being two hours to day,
> But were the day come, I should wish it dark,
> Till I were couching with the doctor's clerk.
> Well, while I live, I'll fear no other thing
> So sore as keeping safe Nerissa's ring.
>
> (V.i. 300–7)

Throughout this scene the Belmont world has been
greying into mundanity: the 'floor of heaven' initially 'thick
inlaid with patines of bright gold' loses its colour as the
moon disappears, and the scene chills into the sterility of
pre-dawn light:

> This night methinks is but the daylight sick;
> It looks a little paler; 'tis a day
> Such as the day is when the sun is hid.
>
> (V.i. 124–6)

Now 'It is almost morning', 'being two hours to day', and
these characters are up too late. The lives left on stage now
seem not rich in potential but unfinished and uncertain in
future meaning. Following the typical pattern of this play, a
final celebration has been promised only to be withheld, and

we are not too disappointed to be excluded from the ordinariness of further converse to be conducted off stage:

> *Portia*　　　　　　　　　　　It is almost morning,
> And yet I am sure you are not satisfied
> Of these events at full. Let us go in,
> And charge us there upon inter'gatories,
> And we will answer all things faithfully.
>
> 　　　　　　　　　　　　　　　(V.i. 295–9)

Perhaps Antonio is so noticeable in these last moments because his characteristic mood is now the atmosphere of the play itself:

> In sooth, I know not why I am so sad.
> It wearies me; you say it wearies you . . .

Afterword: Prejudice and Interpretation

The play's last moments appear to return us to its opening, and, in a sense, invite us to attend yet again to its particularities, puzzles and peculiarities. This study has been written in the belief that this kind of attention is worthwhile. The book has attempted to be open to the play's many diverging interpretative possibilities. And it has been aggressive in its refusal to offer any single 'new' interpretation of the play. Above all, it has sought to ask *questions* about *The Merchant of Venice*; and has sought to say something new about the extensiveness of the play's own questionings and about the dramatic skills deployed in generating such questions.

But some recent criticial theorists clamour to remind us that no critical writing can be *fully* open, 'innocent', devoid of larger predetermining assumptions. *This* news is not new; *The Merchant of Venice* itself can teach us that we are all—of necessity and for good or ill—prejudiced, predisposed, foreknowing. For a variety of reasons, the body of this Introduction resists *explicit* engagement with recent theories. Some of the reasons are mundane; others are of a generality and complexity which can only be adumbrated here. The debate between theory and practice has long been a hackneyed one. The tendentious slide in the use of the word 'theory' itself—between 'theory' as larger implicit

131

assumptions and predispositions underlying practice, and
'theory' as a fully explicit, systematic and coherent account
of literature and language—has long been diagnosed. And
the once heated debate about whether theory should
precede practice or practice precede theory has revealed
itself as a non-question—theory and practice are
inseparable. But, for obvious practical reasons, a short
critical work must choose to privilege either explicit
theoretical issues or sustained consideration of a specific
work. And thus, in accordance with the emphasis of this
series, this Introduction offers itself primarily as a study of
The Merchant of Venice. Moreover, since critical
bouleversements are the order of the day, I should say that I
find what *The Merchant of Venice* has to say about recent
theoretical developments more interesting that what the
new criticisms have to say about the play. Hence I have
chosen to confine such discussion to an Afterword.

   First, it should be said bluntly that the assumption, which
often attends recent critical discussion, that only 'new'
interpretations emanating from 'new' theoretical positions
are of interest, is simply crass and bullying. (On the crass
and bullying, *The Merchant of Venice* is an eloquent
commentary.) Recent critics often assume a naïve progress
in the evolution of literary and cultural criticism which their
own advertised socio-political stances would vehemently
deny to developments in other areas of human life. What
Hazlitt, writing in the early nineteenth century has to say
about *The Merchant of Venice* does not lose interest merely
because it is—in that loaded term—'dated'. Conversely the
'new' is never as new as it might claim. In *Truth and Method*
Hans-Georg Gadamer writes:

> only what is new, or what is planned, appears as the result
> of reason. But this is an illusion. Even where life changes
> violently, as in ages of revolution, far more of the old is
> preserved in the supposed transformation of everything
> than anyone knows, and combines with the new to create

a new value. At any rate, preservation is as much a freely-chosen action as revolution and renewal.

(Gadamer 1979, p. 250)

There is a second, mundane reason why this Introduction has had little to say explicitly about the play and recent theoretical developments. It is simply that *The Merchant of Venice* has not attracted the kinds and prolixity of attention that other Renaissance plays have enjoyed. The play often receives only tangential treatment in the course of wider theorizings and more general considerations of Shakespeare. The little 'new' criticism which has addressed itself specifically to *The Merchant of Venice* to date has proved itself unimpressive on its own terms. Perhaps this is merely a matter of time, and better 'new' interpretations will soon pour forth. Perhaps, on the other hand, *The Merchant of Venice* will show itself as resistant to 'new' interpretation as it has proved to 'old'. I would not deny that any critical practice, including my own, makes large general assumptions. In discussing *The Merchant of Venice* I begin, like the characters themselves, 'in the middle'. But I have yet to find any of the theoretical approaches currently on offer persuasive, and this remains true whether I choose one such approach or attempt to combine a range of them. It is thus not for me to 'invent' new readings of *The Merchant of Venice* in the light of recent theoretical approaches. Indeed, to do so would be disingenuous or—to change idiom—an act of bad faith. Furthermore, any 'inventions' I might manage would be prejudiced in the worst sense, since I am predisposed to find them wanting. They would prove too easy a target.

In *Power on Display*, Leonard Tennenhouse offers a New Historicist reading of *The Merchant of Venice* which concerns itself with the ideology of literary forms and the relation between erotic desire and economic and social power. Tennenhouse sees the romance of the casket test as intimately related to the peculiarly Elizabethan problem which locates power in the female aristocrat, most notably the Queen. The caskets challenge the courtiers to value Portia in respect of her aristocratic blood, a challenge which Bassanio alone meets. Portia gives herself and her power to Bassanio, she confers her patronage on him, in Act 3, scene ii, because of 'his fidelity to the idea that power flows strictly from her'. But 'the words of the aristocratic Portia conspicuously lack the power to constitute . . . a totalizing [social] order', since the mercantile language of Venice immediately encroaches on the courtly discourse of Belmont with news of Antonio's troubles. That mercantile language figures a social order and system of patronage based on male bonding and economic contract rather than sexual exchange. Venetian discourse thus incorporates a larger social order than the courtly discourse of Belmont; in Tennenhouse's terms, it appropriates 'the signs and symbols of the grotesque body and the aristocratic body as well' (Tennenhouse 1986, p. 56).

Shylock, 'the very embodiment of mercantile logic', is opposed to both bodies:

> [Shylock] uses the principle of scarcity against the insatiable hunger of the grotesque body. He also uses the principle of profit against the largesse of the patronage system. Both figures represent corporate bodies, their power deriving from the metaphysics of blood and the desires of the flesh respectively. By way of contrast, Shylock seeks to individuate the collective body, to substitute profit for metaphysics, and to convert flesh into gold. (ibid., p. 57)

The power of mercantile language, embodied in Shylock, is overthrown by 'unruly women', Jessica and Portia; and the latter's strategy of disguise serves 'the means of authorising a traditional [Venetian] hierarchy' (ibid., p. 56). Shylock's defeat—and here Tennenhouse seems grossly to distort the play's own dramatic emphasis—'only clears the stage for this other, more primary symbolic struggle [between the language of patronage relations in Belmont and the language of patronage relations in Venice]' (ibid., p. 59). Portia resolves this struggle and functions as a kind of unruly pun, combining the courtly language of the aristocratic lady with the ribaldry more usual in the low-life women of, for example, earlier fabliaux traditions. Through the ring plot, Portia unites 'the desired object of Bassanio's courtly speech in Belmont' and 'the patron of Bassanio's patron in Venice' (ibid., p. 60). Finally, then, Shakespeare's play vindicates the metaphysics of blood in the figure of Portia.

My summary cannot but misrepresent Tennenhouse's interpretation, and his idiom is all too easily mocked in the name of the now problematic commonsense. But his reading does seem a case of annexing the obvious in the play in order to argue the perverse. In so far as Tennenhouse allows the play to do more than 'display', it emerges as a work of conservatism beyond the wildest dreams of an E. M. W. Tillyard at his most patriotic. And, even if we accept Tennenhouse's peculiar characterisation of the play's various struggles, Tennenhouse seems content to see these struggles convincingly *resolved* by the various tricks with casket codes, legal quibbles, and bawdy puns on rings. The implied credulity of Shakespeare and his Elizabethan audiences seems beyond belief, and contrary to the internal evidence of the play itself, which works so often to provoke an awareness of its plots' troubling improbabilities. Moreover, Tennenhouse's interpretation seems humourlessly schematic in a way that *The Merchant of Venice* itself— in its *odd* use of maxims, aphorisms, symbols and allegories—mocks and problematizes. On the casket test in particular, Tennenhouse seems strikingly vulnerable, if only because he seems unwilling to take account of other different, and perhaps more plausible, interpretations. Tennenhouse conducts his argument at a level of abstraction which holds off from the particulars of the play—'In Shylock's service Gobbo is kept hungry, and

Shylock only agrees to release him to join Bassanio's household with the expectation that Gobbo's habits will sap the strength of its aristocratic largesse' (ibid., p. 56); Gobbo, one feels, will be in need of a very large appetite. Tennenhouse makes rapid, underargued equations (Shylock = 'the very embodiment of mercantile logic' (ibid., p. 56)), which short-circuit the dramatic experience of the play; and, in the particular case of Shylock, as we shall see, the Jew can just as readily be equated with feudalism.

In *Power on Display* Tennenhouse generates an elaborate interpretative structure and then, unsurprisingly if depressingly, demonstrates how *The Merchant of Venice* conforms to, and confirms that larger interpretation. It seems as if Tennenhouse confidently *answers* the interpretative questions of the play before *The Merchant of Venice* is allowed to pose them. And this may be in part because of Tennenhouse's predilection to regard the play as display and spectacle rather than interrogative drama. The structures of understanding which Tennenhouse proffers are a greal deal more sophisticated than the 'facts' of old-fashioned historicism, but their sophistication renders them no less questionable. His interpretation will win favour only with the converted or the easily coerced; *The Merchant of Venice* itself is more resilient and recalcitrant.

Terry Eagleton's recent materialist reading of *The Merchant of Venice* ʼoverlaps to an unsurprisingly large extent with many of interpretative possibilities I have described in the preceding chapters: on the complex relation of the spirit and letter of the law; on the *need* which Shylock, and the victimised and oppressed generally, have of the law's protection; on the possibility that the Christians' capacity for love and mercy may be a luxury available only to those with wealth and in power; and on literalism and extravagance of metaphor in expression (Eagleton 1986, pp. 35–48). But it is also unsurprising that Eagleton is either silent about, or attempts brusquely to nullify, many other possibilities to which I have also called attention. Eagleton's is an interventive and selective strategy. He feels no compunction to attend to the *experience* of the play as it unfolds nor, indeed, to the many other recalcitrant details of any moment he chooses for attention. Thus Eagleton is prepared to enter the Venetian courtroom rather late in the proceedings:

> Shylock is triumphantly vindicated even though he loses the case: he has forced the Christians into outdoing his own 'inhuman' legalism. Indeed it is tempting to speculate that Shylock never really expected to win in the first place; he is hardly well placed to do so, as a solitary, despised outsider confronting a powerful, clubbish ruling class. One can imagine him waiting with a certain academic interest to see what dodge the Christians will devise to let one of their own kind off the hook. Perhaps he throws the audience a knowing wink when Portia produces her knockdown argument.
>
> (ibid., pp. 37–8)

Temptation is always hard to resist, especially when its reward is the kind of sentimentalised Shylock we are already all too familiar with in accounts of *The Merchant of Venice*. But the importation of a Brechtian wink to alienate—or perhaps to insulate—the audience from engagement with so many of the other things which are going on in the Venetian courtroom does suggest that Eagleton is reading, and needs to be reading, a play much closer to Wesker's *The Merchant* than Shakespeare's *The Merchant of Venice*.

In Shakespeare's play, Antonio does not know why he is so sad, and Solanio, Salerio and Gratiano are none too successful in finding an explanation. The fast-moving Eagleton, with a little help from Freud and Marx, has no such difficulties:

> Melancholy, as Freud wrote, is mourning without an object: founded on some lack or loss, it pervades the

whole of one's experience but, because apparently causeless, seems at the same time a pure void ... Melancholy is much ado about nothing, a blank, motiveless devaluation of the world. The less its cause can be identified the more acute the condition grows, feeding on its own indeterminacy; and the more acute the condition, the less definable its grounds. We have already seen such paradoxes of 'all' and 'nothing' associated in Shakespeare with money, and it is thus not accidental that Antonio is not only melancholic but a merchant— indeed *the* Merchant—of Venice. Melancholia is an appropriate neurosis for a profit-based society, discarding the use values of objects in order to plunder them for substance with which to nourish itself.

(ibid., pp. 40–41)

In earlier chapters I have suggested that Portia's and Bassanio's love may be a luxury. Holding the Belmont scenes at arms length, as it were, Eagleton denies that this love is love at all:

there is nothing surprising in the way that this self-loving parasite [Bassanio] then elevates love over riches in the very act of purchasing a woman. Such romanticism, with its sanctimonious talk of the inestimability of love, is just the other side of the commercial coin: the bourgeoisie have always pretended that sex transcends utility, at the very moment they debase it to a commodity. The Romantic is in this respect just the flipside of the Utilitarian, fetishizing a realm (the love of a good woman) supposedly free of his own squalid transactions. 'The bourgeois viewpoint,' Marx comments, 'has never advanced beyond this antithesis between itself and this romantic viewpoint, and therefore the latter will accompany it as its legitimate antithesis up to its blessed end.'

(ibid., pp. 45–6)

The vehemence, the rhetorical patterning ('. . . just . . . just
. . .'), the reductive and driven single-mindedness, and the
citing of holy writ have all been anticipated in the words of
Antonio and Shylock in the third scene of *The Merchant of
Venice*—the critic is thus 'placed' by the play. 'New'
interpretations, no less than 'old', seem here unable to
escape the censure of the play's own larger diverging
perspectives.

Turning from Terry Eagleton to Catherine Belsey, one
might be forgiven for deducing that cultural materialism and
feminism are at loggerheads over *The Merchant of Venice*.
Thus Belsey sees Shakespeare intent on disrupting sexual
difference to secure a new and better notion of the feminine,
and celebrates the liberation of Portia's disguise where
'Portia fights Bassanio's legal battle for him—and wins.'
(Belsey in Drakakis (ed.) 1985, p. 179). Portia is thus allowed
to unite the virtues of love and hitherto exclusively
masculine friendship in a new definition of marriage which
allows her to be lover, partner and companion. But we do
not need Eagleton to remind us that this battle in the
Venetian courtroom is a dubious one, to say the least, and
that Portia's victory over Shylock is secured at great cost.
Moreover, Belsey's thesis is rendered more problematic,
since Portia's legal tricks derive from the unseen presence of
the patriarch, Bellario. Belsey herself glimpses another
feminist-orientated reading which might well argue that the
play shows the gender of Portia disguised and thereby
conveniently denied merely so that she may be exploited to
further the aims of patriarchal Venice. And, if Portia unites
the values of love and friendship in the bond plot, her
actions in the ring plot might be seen to set such values in
opposition—forcing Bassanio to choose between marriage
and friendship. Again, whether Portia's tricky resolution of
the ring plot is to be read as an agreeable conclusion or an
obfuscation is open to question. (My own account of the
ring plot in Act 5 of the play—that it is unsettled, ambiguous
and insufficiently realised—may be judgemental, but it

seems preferable to any single interpretative appropriation or importation.) To be fair to Belsey, her approach is more convincingly substantial and detailed in her analyses of *As You Like It* and *Twelfth Night*, and she recognises the limitations and potential contradictions of her own reading of *The Merchant of Venice*:

> Portia's right to exercise her authority depends on her lawyer's robes, and the episode can be seen as making visible the injustice which allows women authority only on condition that they seem to be men. Even while it reaffirms patriarchy, the tradition of female transvestism challenges it precisely by unsettling the categories which legitimate it.
>
> (ibid., p. 180)

Once more a reading of *The Merchant of Venice* which foregrounds a radical aim must either be partial in the literal sense of selecting only parts of the text for attention, or risk complication and contradiction. And thus it may be telling, rather than accidental, that feminist criticisms as diverse as those of Juliet Dusinberre in *Shakespeare and the Nature of Women* (1975) and the large selection in *The Woman's Part: Feminist Criticism of Shakespeare* (Lenz et. al. (eds.) 1980) all give *The Merchant of Venice* only incidental and piecemeal consideration.

Those with the assurance to sift their prejudices, confident enough to distinguish between good and bad, can transform prejudice into overtly declared political commitments and can then *use* the Shakespearean text to further their radical political ends, 'adjusting Shakespeare to radical ends' as Alan Sinfield has it (Sinfield in Dollimore and Sinfield eds. 1985, p. 178). But others do not enjoy such confidence, and are provoked into scepticism, scepticism often uncomfortably sharpened by repeated experience of Shakespeare's plays. And this experience of Shakespeare is not the one-way process that radicals' use and adjustment imply; in the course of such experience Shakespeare may change us as we change Shakespeare. While it may be legitimate to use Shakespeare to further radical ends, we might recall that the trial scene of *The Merchant of Venice* makes its own comment on ends justifying means. Moreover, the Shakespearean text may prove something of a Trojan horse in *any* single political citadel, not because Shakespeare transcends history and politics, but because his works problematise them. The multiplying and complicating perspectives on love and friendship, usury, mercantile ventures, and capitalism in *The Merchant of Venice* suggest the more general proposition that the oppositional model, favoured by recent radical critics, between the 'Establishment' and the 'Radical' may be a necessary strategy for such radicals but may also involve over-simplification. We have been encouraged to talk of pluralism, and of the Shakespearean text's patience before its many interpreters; perhaps we might now consider scepticism, and the Shakespearean text's resistance to interpretative appropriation.

Throughout this study I have attempted to show that the play returns its characters repeatedly to the searching questions of who and what they are. Shakespeare is much exercised in *The Merchant of Venice* with questions about the nature of the self. Throughout the play we are never allowed to see individual identity as something apart from the highly particularised social, political and economic conditions of its Venetian and Belmont worlds. But nor are we allowed to explain individual behaviour as *merely* the consequence of such conditions. The play's great challenge lies in the moments when it asks its audiences to sustain a kind of double vision—to see the inner lives of individuals *and* to see the social and political conditions, which shape and are shaped by such inner lives. Shakespeare's dramatic skills work precisely to that end; he combines the stock figures and conventions of comedy with what I might call his habit of interiorisation, the creation of a dramatic language which confers an 'inner life' on the characters he finds in his sources. Consequently, we are at times simultaneously invited to look inward to individual psychology, and outward to social and political conditions. This puzzle transfers itself to interpreters of *The Merchant of Venice*. In this study I have called attention to various moments in the play where we are uncertain whether we are watching and hearing a highly individualised character or a type, a stock-type, a stereotype; and I have suggested something of the different directions interpretation might take depending on which view an interpreter might take. Much criticism of *The Merchant of Venice* has been concerned with character-study. More recently we have been asked to turn from character to explanations in terms of ideology, the various power relations existing between the various groups in the play. Each approach can seem, on occasion, an over-reading, and, on occasion, an impoverishment of the play. Interpreters predisposed to assuming the autonomy of human identity will be content to talk of individual psychology and to offer character analysis. Interpreters predisposed to thinking in terms of ideology will offer analysis in terms of larger social, political and economic conditions and forces. Each predisposition forecloses engagement with the great challenge, which *The Merchant of Venice* so often works to produce, and each will find the familiar and agreeable only at the cost of losing what is other and unsettling in the play.

Much of my argument in this 'Afterword' has been anticipated, though in very different terms and terms more sympathetic to recent revisionist criticisms, by Walter Cohen in an article, '*The Merchant of Venice* and the Possibilities of Historical Criticism' (1982). Here Cohen tests numerous possible historical interpretations against the play in painstaking and sympathetic detail. Cohen begins by viewing the play in the context of sixteenth-century England, with Shylock as the embodiment of capitalism in opposition to the aristocrat and the venturing merchant. But Cohen notes that in England merchants were also the leading usurers and 'suspicion of Italian traders ran particularly high' (Cohen 1982, p. 769). Cohen also recognizes that the play is broadly procapitalist 'at least as far as commerce is concerned' (ibid., p. 768), and that Shakespeare deviates from sixteenth-century English realities in the play's Venetian setting and in respect of Shylock's religion. Attempts to Anglicize Shylock allegorically fail because, while he has traits in common with both the stereotypical grasping Puritan *and* the Catholic (itself something of a contradiction!), Shylock is 'too complex and contradictory' to fit any sixteenth-century English stereotype. Cohen thus turns to late sixteenth-century Venice only to find the historical details again at odds with Shakespeare's play: Jewish usurers were barred from the city, and Jews worked as merchants. Taking a longer historical perspective, Cohen does indeed find, in medieval Italy, Jewish usurers in the context of a rising mercantile class among the Christians. Seen from this perspective, Antonio embodies rising capitalism in opposition to the decaying feudalism embodied in Shylock. Shylock is now not a new threat but 'an old man with obsolete values trying to arrest the course of history' (ibid., p. 771). Antonio too becomes an ambiguous figure:

> As a traditional and conservative figure, he nearly becomes a tragic victim of economic change; as the embodiment of progressive forces, he points toward the comic resolution.
>
> (ibid., p. 772)

Cohen concludes that 'in *The Merchant of Venice* English history evokes fears of capitalism, and Italian history allays those fears' (ibid., p. 772).

Undaunted, the critic turns to Marx's various writings on usury, merchants and Jews. Marx is shown often to equate capitalism and Judaism. But in discussing usury, Marx argues that usury predates capitalism and declines with the transition to mercantile capitalism, the latter prefiguring industrial capitalism. And Cohen further reveals that Marx, in discussing how *industrial* capitalism continually threatens to deprive labour of its instruments of labour, appropriates Shylock's 'you take my life/When you do take the means whereby I live' (IV.i. 371–2), thus implicitly identifying the Christians with capitalism and Shylock with labour. Shylock, in the light of Marx's writings remains a shifting and ambiguous figure: 'Marx's use of selective quotation succeeds in capturing Shylock as both victimizer and victim' (ibid., p. 773).

Cohen gives similar though briefer attention to the issues of law, the country and the city, and love in *The Merchant of Venice*, with similar results. He concludes that the complexity of the play 'is a consequence of fundamental contradiction in Shakespeare's social material' and that we are able 'to understand and in a sense to justify the opposed responses to *The Merchant of Venice*, to see in its flaws not signs of artistic incompetence but manifestations of preformal problems' (ibid., p. 774). Shakespeare's chosen form—romantic comedy—proves inadequate in resolving the preformal problems: 'Some of the merit of *The Merchant of Venice* ironically lies in the failure of its central design to provide a completely satisfying resolution to the dilemmas raised in the course of the action' (ibid., p. 775).

And what does Cohen see as the consequences of such a conclusion for interpretations of the play? We must avoid 'a complicity of silence with the play, in which the ideology of the form is uncritically reproduced and the whole, *The Merchant of Venice* as we have it, is replaced by the part' (ibid., p. 775). But nor must we ignore the 'positive value of Shakespeare's comedy', the attempted but not entirely successful celebratory resolution, since escapism is also liberation:

the play persistently attempts to establish a congruence

between economic and moral conduct, between outer and inner wealth; to depict a society in which human relationships are not exploitative. Such a vision, quite literally a fantasy, simultaneously distracts us from the deficiencies of our lives and reveals to us the possibility of something better.

(ibid., pp. 775–6)

Cohen's mode of discourse may differ from my own, but our conclusions are not dissimilar. We have returned, by a circuitous route, to the twin dangers of the Scylla of under-readings, emphasising celebration, and the Charybdis of ingenious over-readings, emphasising irony, which I outlined in the first chapter.

Prejudice seems inescapable. What kind of interpretation should we pursue in such circumstances? In writing about *The Merchant of Venice* I have pursued an exploratory critical method which envisages the encounter between text and interpreter as an exchange of questions, and I have done so in pursuit of an ideal, albeit an unattainable ideal, of non-appropriative interpretation. In writing 'Only a person who has questions can have knowledge' (Gadamer 1979, p. 328), Gadamer puts the position at its most extreme:

The isolation of a prejudice clearly requires the suspension of its validity for us. For so long as our mind is influenced by a prejudice, we do not know and consider it as a judgment. How then are we able to isolate it? It is impossible to make ourselves aware of it while it is constantly operating unnoticed, but only when it is, so to speak, stimulated. The encounter with a text from the past can provide this stimulus . . . Understanding begins . . . when something addresses us . . .

The essence of the question is the opening up, and keeping open of possiblities.

(ibid., p. 266)

Doubtless, in the course of this study, too many possibilities have remained closed, but the exchange of questions between *The Merchant of Venice* and this particular spectator and reader, while unsettling at times, remains unfinished and continues to seem worthwhile.

Bibliography

EDITIONS OF *THE MERCHANT OF VENICE*

Brown, John Russell (ed.), *The New Arden* revised edition (London, 1961).

Furness, H. H. (ed.), *The New Variorum* (Philadelphia, 1888).

Mahood, M. M. (ed.), *The New Cambridge* (Cambridge, 1987).

Merchant, W. Moelwyn (ed.), *The New Penguin* (Harmondsworth, 1967).

Myrick, Kenneth (ed.), *The Signet* (New York, 1965).

Quiller-Couch, A., and Dover Wilson, J. (eds.), *The Cambridge* (Cambridge, 1926).

CRITICISM AND OTHER WORKS

Bacon, Francis, *The Essays*, 1625 edition, ed. by John Pitcher (Harmondsworth, 1985).

Barber, C. L., *Shakespeare's Festive Comedy* (first published, 1959; Princeton, NJ, 1972).

Berry, Ralph, *Shakespeare's Comedies: Explorations in Form* (Princeton, NJ, 1972).

Berry, Ralph, *Shakespeare and the Awareness of the Audience* (London, 1985).

Bradbury, Malcolm, and David Palmer (eds.), *Shakespearian Comedy*, Stratford upon Avon Studies 14 (London, 1972).

Bradley, A. C., *Shakespearean Tragedy* (first published 1904; London, 1976).

Bradshaw, Graham, 'The Merchant of Venice: Does Jessica lie?' *Meridian* 5 (1986) 99–108.

Brown, John Russell and Bernard Harris (eds.), *Early Shakespeare* Stratford upon Avon Studies 3 (London, 1961).

Brown, John Russell, *Shakespeare and His Comedies* (London, 1962).

Bullough, Geoffrey, *Narrative and Dramatic Sources of Shakespeare*, Vol. 1 (London, 1957).

Charlton, H. B., *Shakespearian Comedy* (first published 1938; London, 1949).

Cohen, D. M., 'The Jew and Shylock', *Shakespeare Quarterly* 31 (1980) 53-63.

Cohen, Walter, 'The Merchant of Venice and the Possibilities of Historical Criticism', *ELH* 49 (1982) 765–89.

Dollimore, Jonathan and Alan Sinfield (eds.), *Political Shakespeare: New Essays in Cultural Materialism* (Manchester, 1985).

Drakakis, John (ed.), *Alternative Shakespeares* (London and New York, 1985).

Dusinberre, Juliet, *Shakespeare and the Nature of Women* (London, 1975).

Eagleton, Terry, *William Shakespeare* (Oxford and New York, 1986).

Eliot, T. S., *Selected Essays* (first published 1932; London, 1951).

Gadamer, Hans-Georg, *Truth and Method* (first published in English 1975; London, 1979).

Goddard, Harold C., *The Meaning of Shakespeare*, Vol. 1

(first published 1951; Chicago, 1960).

Granville-Barker, Harley, *Prefaces to Shakespeare*, Vol. 1, (first published 1930; London, 1958).

Hazlitt, William, *Characters of Shakespeare's Plays* (first published 1817; London, 1955).

Leggatt, Alexander, *Shakespeare's Comedies of Love* (London, 1974).

Lenz, Carolyn Ruth Swift, Gayle Greene and Carol Thomas Neely (eds.), *The Woman's Part: Feminist Criticism of Shakespeare* (Urbana, Illinois, 1980).

Lewalski, Barbara K., 'Biblical Allusion and Allegory in *The Merchant of Venice*', *Shakespeare Quarterly* 13 (1962) pp.327-43.

Moody, A.D., *Shakespeare: 'The Merchant of Venice'* (London, 1964).

Nevo, Ruth, *Comic Transformations in Shakespeare's Plays* (London, 1980).

Nuttall, A.D., *A New Mimesis: Shakespeare and the Representation of Reality* (London, 1983).

Rabkin, Norman, *Shakespeare and the Problem of Meaning* (Chicago, 1981).

Rees, Joan, *Shakespeare and the Story* (London, 1978).

Spencer, Christopher (ed.), *Five Restoration Adaptions of Shakespeare* (Urbana, Illinois, 1965).

Stoll, E.E., *Shakespeare Studies* (New York, 1927).

Tennenhouse, Leonard, *Power on Display: The Politics of Shakespeare's Genres* (New York and London, 1986).

Wesker, Arnold, *The Merchant* (first published, 1977; London, 1983).

Wilders, John (ed.), *'The Merchant of Venice': A Casebook* (London, 1969).

Wilson, Thomas, *A Discourse Upon Usury* (first published 1572), with an Introduction by R.H. Tawney (London, 1962).

Index